My Life's Greatest Troubles

Vernon T. Smith Sr.

This book is written from the author's personal experience and perspective. In the text that follows, many people's and company's names and identifying characteristics have been changed, so that any resemblance to actual living or dead, events, companies or locales is entirely coincidental.

Copyright © 2023 Vernon T. Smith Sr

My Life's Greatest Troubles
By Vernon T. Smith Sr.

Printed in the United States of America

ISBN # 978-1-959667-22-3

All rights reserved solely by the author. The author guarantees all contents are original and do not infringe upon the legal rights of any other person or work. No part of this book may be reproduced in any form without the permission of the author. The view expressed in this book are not necessarily those of the publisher.

www.paprovipublishing.com

My Life's Greatest Troubles

Table of Contents

Dedication

Introduction	Page 1
Chapter One	Page 5
Chapter Two	Page 15
Chapter Three	Page 23
Chapter Four	Page 35
Chapter Five	Page 41
Chapter Six	Page 47
Chapter Seven	Page 53
Chapter Eight	Page 60
Chapter Nine	Page 64
Chapter Ten	Page 77
Chapter Eleven	Page 82
Chapter Twelve	Page 92
Chapter Thirteen	Page 98
Epilogue	Page 111
About the Author	Page 115

DEDICATION

This book is dedicated to my mother, Mrs. Helen Louis Glass Smith. You mean everything to me. Thank you for loving us unconditionally.

To my first love Diana.

I want you to know that I never forgot about you. Words cannot express how deeply sorry I am for the pain I caused you. I never meant to break your heart. I pray every day that you have found it within your own heart to forgive me. My only excuse is being young and not recognizing that actions in young love have consequences. I hope you read this book and see that my words are sincere. I hope life has served you well and you are happy! God Bless You!

INTRODUCTION

This book is not intended to discredit anyone in any shape, form, or fashion. It is strictly about my life. "My Life's Greatest Troubles" Part One is about me, a little boy growing up in the mid '70s and early '80s, it's about being raised up by a single parent, my mother, Mrs. Helen. It's about my life as a young boy along with my other siblings and how we were able to survive, in spite of hardships.

This book is about my life as a young boy growing up with my younger brother and how we continued to exist despite not having a father guiding us or showing us true values. It's about what happens when there is no father around making sure we understood the importance of how to pray before bed and to tuck us under the covers before we go to sleep at night. Psalms 91:4 He will cover you with his feathers and under his wings you will find refuge. Being safe and sheltered from danger and trouble, we never knew anything about that.

I can remember how me and my baby brother stood in the driveway waiting for our father. We would count and point our fingers at the cars as they went by. I would say, that's my car! Then my brother would say no, that's my car! We would say that as we waited on our father to come, but he never showed up. I also remember hearing my mother and my older sister as a little boy, saying, now I lay me down to sleep, I pray the Lord my soul to keep and if I should die before I wake, I pray to God my soul to take.

  My Life Greatest Trouble talks about when I first started Kindergarten, at Minnie S. Howell Elementary School. I can remember my mother taking me to school and picking me up from school. Most of the time we walked to the PTA meetings, the school plays, to sports and other events in the school. It was always my mama, no male figures... not even an older brother. I was fatherless! I was fatherless when it came to raising up a child in the way he should go and teaching him to see God's wisdom and will for abilities and talents.

My Life's Greatest Troubles

Minnie S. Howell Elementary School now serving as the headquarters for Premier Academy

I thank God for the many talents in my life. For example, I remember as a little boy around 11 years old, my older sister Bonita (Neet) used to watch us, me and my baby brother Byron (Byeboo), while our mother was at work during the summer. One day I told my sister that I was hungry. She says to me, Vernon cook you something to eat, cook you some breakfast...so I did. I cooked eggs, bacon, grits, and toast. It was so good! I thank my sister for showing me and giving me that opportunity to learn at a young age. Guess what? It paid off! I am one-of-a-kind in the kitchen today. My desire is to one day own a Soul Food Restaurant.

My Life's greatest troubles talks about my grandparents on my father's side of the family and how they inspired me. I thank God for them being a part of my life but most of all how God is the omnipotence, omniscience, and omnipresent God, even in the time of trouble. "My Life's Greatest

My Life's Greatest Troubles

Troubles" talks about how sometimes you can find yourself in trouble you put yourself in and nobody to blame but you. Regardless of that, God is our refuge and strength, a very an ever-present help in trouble Psalm 46:1. I can go on and on talking about "My Life's Greatest Troubles" but I need to stop to give you enough time to grab a bag of chips and dip and a soda to enjoy this true book by yours truly, Vernon Torrance Smith Sr. "My Life Greatest Troubles" Part 2 will pick back up in the year 1993. Get ready, it is going to take a twist and some turns.

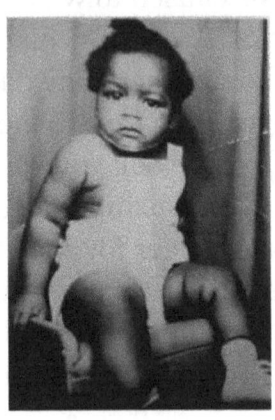
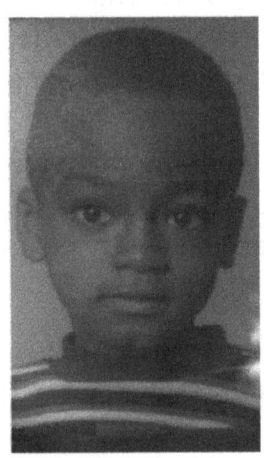

CHAPTER 1

*M*y name is Vernon Torrance Smith Sr. I was born on August 1, 1964, to Mr. Harold Lewis Smith and Miss Helen Louise Glass Smith in Atlanta, Georgia at Grady Hospital. I am six of eight children: Greg, Bonita, Phyllis, Anthony (deceased), Giselle, Me, Byron, Tawana (deceased). I attended Minnie S. Howell Elementary, Crawford Long Middle, and Walter F. George High schools. Since I did not finish high school, I received my GED.

I lived at 3292 Jonesboro Rd, SE Atlanta, GA. I grew up in a place called Macedonia. My grandmother was Mrs. Lucille Colvin Smith Hambrick born on August 5, 1908. She was the oldest daughter to Timothy and Alice Kemp Colvin. She married Idres

My Life's Greatest Troubles

Smith. They had two children named Harold and Colvin She later married Rubin Hambrick. She was a graduate of Booker T. Washington High School.

My grandmother went on to receive a bachelor's degree of Science from Fort Valley State College and then a master's degree of Art from Atlanta University. She became a teacher at W.A. Fountain School in Clayton County. We called my grandmother Mamacile and my grandfather Daddy Rubin. They lived across the street from me and my uncle Colvin, (my dad's brother) Bubba, and my aunt Marie and their daughter Shawna lived next door.

My grandparents' house is still standing after more than 70 years.

My first job was at the Thrift Town Grocery Store in Blair Village, bagging groceries for $3.15 an hour plus tips. My job was to bag the groceries and take them to the car for the customers. Those were the good old days. After that, I started working for the

My Life's Greatest Troubles

Holiday Inn in Forest Park, GA as a busboy cleaning tables and assisting with room service. During that time, I joined the Ephesus Baptist Church under Rev. M. Davis on Wylie Street in SE Atlanta, where I was baptized in the late 70's.

My grandparents were special to me. Growing up in the late 70's, and being around my grandparents, I learned so much from them. My grandad, Daddy Rubin, was born on August 19, 1904, in Henry County. He was a deacon at the Zion Grove Baptist Church in Ellenwood, GA. He was a praying man and a great man of God. One day we were talking and he told me that he never went to school. I could not believe it because watching him when he took me to work with him, he knew everything. I was his labor boy, giving him his tools as he asked for them, he even paid me.

Daddy Rubin was a carpenter, a plumber, an electrician, and a contractor. You name it he did it. I believe he was gifted by God Himself. He had many other gifts that included being a barber. He had his own barbershop down the hill beside his house on Jonesboro Road. People came from all around town to get a haircut, especially on Fridays and Saturdays when he did the one of a kind special.

Daddy Rubin also built houses, he even built the house I was born and raised in. This was my grandparents' house before they moved across the

My Life's Greatest Troubles

street to 3265 Jonesboro Road. Daddy Rubin owned houses in Ellenwood that he rented out. I can remember riding with him to collect his rent money.

He taught me so much. He taught me how to fish and hunt. He even taught me how to drive a straight shift Chevy Pickup C10 long bed green 1968 truck. I remember him even teaching me how to shoot his 410 12-gauge shotgun. He also had a 22 long Rifle which I had a lot of fun with. I could not wait for squirrel season in September so that I could shoot them out of the top of the tree before they jumped to the next tree. I used to hit them in the air sometimes. Yes sir, I loved to go hunting in Conley GA for those squirrels. I will never forget those good old days.

Daddy Rubin had a Beagle hunting dog for rabbit season, and his name was "Joe." Daddy Rubin said he was the best. We would load the truck up with "Joe" and our guns, and off we went hunting. We would go from Stockbridge to Ellenwood, and sometimes we would go to the side creek in Blair Village/Poole Creek. He would turn the Beagle loose so they could pick up the rabbit scent on the trail, and I would watch them go. LOL. "Joe" would start howling, and Daddy Rubin would say, "go get 'em," and the dogs would all be howling. I was laughing because it was so funny when Grandad would start howling like the dogs.

My Life's Greatest Troubles

They would run the rabbits out of the woods into the road, and Daddy Rubin would shoot them when they came onto the road. I had a lot of fun with Daddy Rubin, who also taught me how to build rabbit traps, and I made so many I started selling them for $5 or $10. I made many traps and would set them up to catch rabbits, but all I ever caught were possums, so Grandad kept some in a cage and fed them until he was ready to shoot them, skin them and cook them. He cooked them with sweet potatoes. WOW! My grandad could also play the piano, the guitar, and the harmonica. He could also sew.

Hey, this is going to trip you out. Daddy Rubin made a washing machine that I thought to be unique. Don't ask me how he did this; I remember Mamacile washing clothes next to the garage. Grandad was one of a kind. Remember I told you that he never went to school. I believe that his wisdom and knowledge came from God, and I am so grateful that he allowed me to be in their life and present. They were known throughout the community and all around. Some people never met their grandparents, and in these times today, those who know them are not spending the time they should with them.

Let me tell you, I would be at home, and I could smell Mamacile as she was cooking breakfast and looking out the window and singing. She did not lock her door often, so I would get out of bed and run across the street to her house. She sang, "Pass me not,

My Life's Greatest Troubles

oh gentle savior." Mamacile was cooking up some fatback bacon, grits, and runny eggs with hoecakes. Daddy Rubin loved some runny eggs with Karo syrup and his buttermilk. He also loves to suck raw eggs(wow). I could hear Mamacile calling Daddy Rubin to come and eat, and it was funny because when she called him, the dog, chickens, and cats would start hollering too. Mamacile taught me how to make hoecakes, but mine never came out like Mamacile's.

    I loved it when she sang, "Don't let nobody turn you around, turn you around, turn you round, keep on walking, keep on talking marching to freedom land." As I think about this, it is now 2021, and back in the late 70s; deep down in my soul, I believe that God laid a hand on me and anointed me with oil when I was a young boy around my grandparents. I think it originated from a particular place and time my grandparents went through when they sang around the house. I felt something inside of me that started me singing because of them.

    I remember one summer night when Daddy Rubin was playing around and singing on the piano. My aunt Marie, Homer Griffin, and a friend from down the street were listening to him sing "What a Friend We Have in Jesus," and then he stopped singing and playing. I did not know all the words to the song, but when he stopped, I started singing and finished the song. Grandad hollered out and said that

My Life's Greatest Troubles

I was gonna be a preacher. "Yea, he is gonna be a bad preacher, a bad booger." I kept singing " Hold On Just a Little Longer" when my aunt Marie hollered out that she wanted me to sing that song at her funeral. I asked her why she said that, and she said just in case anything happened to her. I told her nothing was going to happen to her. She then told me that I was her favorite nephew and she loved me, and I told her I loved her back. This was in 1978 or 1979.

My aunt Marie was a very loving and special person with a pure heart. She loved everybody! We sang all the time and had a lot of fun together. She and I would go fishing with Daddy Rubin and Mamacile. One summer, I remember auntie Marie and another person caught the Marta bus #55 Orchard Knob in front of the house and took it to Atlanta Fulton County Stadium to see the Atlanta Braves play. We had a good time because we brought a cooler full of beers and snacks. The Braves lost, but we had so much fun.

My Life's Greatest Troubles

  I remember cutting school with my friend Mark, but sometimes I was by myself, and Aunt Marie would see me in the woods near my grandparent's house, and she would never tell on me. Sometimes she would let me come into her house. Uncle Bubba would be at work with Allied Van Lines. Aunt Marie was my favorite aunt, and I miss her dearly. She is always in my heart.

  When Aunt Marie died in May 1982, my heart was broken and sad because I saw her hours before her passing. She came to my house from next door, and I was lying on the sofa in the living room. Aunt Marie asked me to let her have a few dollars. When I saw her after I got up, I told her she needed to go to the hospital because she had a bad cold, was coughing, and had a super runny nose. I begged her to go to the hospital; that was the last time I could talk with her before she died. That evening I was so sad and scared to go and see her because we were so close, so I did not want to see her dead. I wanted to remember her the way she was. I did not go to the funeral. I chickened out and was afraid because I hurt so much.

  I did not honor her request to sing the song she wanted me to sing at her funeral. I am so sorry that I chickened out. Aunt Marie, please forgive me. I love you, rest in heaven. The first time I sang in public was at Rita's (my wife) grandmother's funeral at the request of Mrs. Angela Elaine Jackson on March 20,

My Life's Greatest Troubles

1994, at the Alexander Memorial AME Church, where I sang "Hold On Just a Little While Longer." I honored my Aunt Marie with that song by choice, and I will never turn anybody else down from a request. I let my Aunt Marie down, and I am still bothered about it to this very day.

I could write an entire book about my grandparents. Mamacile got sick with Alzheimer's disease and passed away in June 1988. Daddy Rubin went blind because he had so many health issues. Daddy Rubin died six months later, in December 1988. May God rest their souls in Heaven (amen). Love you, Mamacile and Daddy Rubin. Thank you for your wisdom and knowledge until we meet again.

My Life's Greatest Troubles

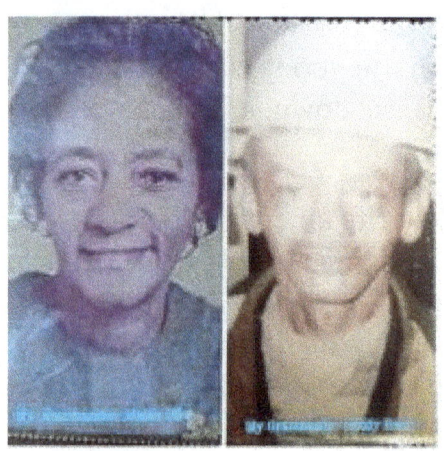

CHAPTER 2

My mother, Mrs. Helen Louise Glass Smith, was born on February 10, 1933, in Waco, GA. Haralson County to Robert and Jalma Norwood Glass. She moved to Atlanta, where she attended school in Atlanta and Clayton County in July 1951 when she was joined in holy matrimony to Harold Lewis Smith. This union produced eight children, four boys, and four girls. They joined Alexander Memorial AME Church in Atlanta, GA., and divorced after 17 years of marriage. My loving mother, Mrs. Helen, worked many jobs. She worked as a housekeeper for the Walkers in Forest Park and for Jefferson Hotel on Pryor and Alabama in Atlanta. She also worked at the Rib at Underground Atlanta and Eastern food near Atlanta International Airport in College Park, and at Pet Bakery on Grant Street in Atlanta. My mother, Mrs. Helen, was a go-getter. She raised my younger brother Byron (called Byeboo) and me.

Mama was our support system throughout our lives in the early 70s. My mother, Mrs. Helen, was a hard worker and provided for her family. I remember being five, and Byeboo was three when I started kindergarten at Minnie Howell. Mama was right there for us and always did the best she could to ensure that we had the necessities to make it. I am sure it was a struggle, but we always made it.

My Life's Greatest Troubles

Let me talk about my Mama, Mrs. Helen, for a little while. She was the best, especially during the holidays. We had a great time when Christmas came around. No matter what we got, and even when we did not get much, sometimes just fruit, apples and oranges, nuts, and some peppermint candy, it was great for all that Mama did. She was magnificent. We lived in the green house on Jonesboro Road. In essence, we were raised in a small house. We referred to it as home but it was known to some people as a

My Life's Greatest Troubles

shotgun house. Love, peace, joy, happiness, and the fruit of the spirit were in that house. We did not care what it looked like because I rather we lived where the spirit was than in a nice house or split-level house where there was no spirit. We were together and grateful in the shotgun shack house.

Let me explain the shotgun house. The shotgun house was a very narrow rectangular frame no more than 10 or 12 feet wide with rooms arranged one behind the other with a door at each end of the house. One room is usually about 12 feet wide and three or four rooms deep. The front door led right into the living room. There were one or two bedrooms and a kitchen in the back and no hallway. That was our house on Jonesboro Road.

Did you notice I did not mention a bathroom? Thanks be to God that Daddy Rubin added a bathroom to the house he built on Jonesboro Road because shotgun houses did not have a bathroom. They had an outhouse in the woods away from the shotgun shack, but we were grateful. When it rained, the house leaked, Mama would get some pots and buckets to catch the leak from the rain, and when it got cold outside, we used to nail plastic to the windows. Mama would go to Ace Hardware store and get plastic, kerosene, candles, lamp oil, and whatever we needed to make sure we could make it through the winter cold.

My Life's Greatest Troubles

We put plastic on the windows and door to keep the cold air out. We had some heaters and a fireplace in the house, but it was still cold, so we would put on more clothes with two or three pairs of socks, whatever we needed to keep warm. Sometimes we would put towels at the door to help keep the draft from coming underneath the bottom of the door. I was eight when the ice storm came in 1973 for two days in January. Sleet and freezing rain fell on January 7th and 8th in 1973, with more than four inches of ice accumulating and causing us to lose power. The temperature dropped below zero, and icicles were hanging from the house. The icicles were taller than me, and school was closed for about one week because there were no lights and it was freezing. Thanks to Mama, we made it through, and I will never forget it.

We never went without food. We may not have always gotten what we wanted to eat, but whatever mama put together, it was good. Let me tell you something my mama would put together. She would take some ground beef and make a s*** on a shank with some roman noodles or potatoes, sweet peas, and cornbread. Man, what you say? It was on and poppin'. Now don't mess around and have some extra sugar and a pack of kool-aid; you would swing like a monkey in a tree. You may be wondering what a s*** on a shank is, so here it is: ground beef scrambled up with onions and bell peppers with mama's homemade gravy with all-purpose flour. I made it sometimes for my children when they were growing up. It was good, but mamas was delicious because she knew how to do it and make enough to feed the whole family(amen). Thank you, God. We sometimes had oatmeal or Cream of Wheat, cornflakes or Special K, and Post Toasties for breakfast. I am talking about the late 60's early 70's.

Children can choose any cereal they want today: Apple Jacks, Fruit Loops, Cinnamon Toast Crunch, Cap'n Crunch, Fruity Pebbles, Honey Nut Cheerios, Frosted Flakes, and Honeycomb. We can't leave out Lucky Charms. Many children are lucky and charmed, telling their parents what they want and don't want to eat. Let me prove it to you. Stop by the grocery store and buy Kellogg Corn Flakes or some Kellogg Rice Krispies or Post Special K. Don't say anything, just put it on the table and leave it there. Most kids would not eat it because they prefer pre-sweetened cereal. We had to put sugar on our cereal back in the day if we had some sugar. If we did not, we would borrow a cup from the neighbors, who were actually my Uncle Bubba and Aunt Marie.

We were family, so if they needed something, they would likewise come and borrow with no problem. It is now 2022, and you cannot borrow anything from anybody, sometimes not even from family. When I was coming up, people looked out for each other; in other words, we helped each other. People were nicer back then. They did not have to

My Life's Greatest Troubles

know you to help. We made milk from powder sometimes, and I am grateful because things got better when Thanksgiving came.

Mama would get the ham, collard greens, blackeye peas, potato salad, turkey and chicken dressing, sweet potato pie, and the upside-down pineapple cake ready. My mama's chicken dressing was the best I have ever eaten. Now, if anybody's chicken dressing comes close to mama's, it's mine. Yes, sir, I believe my sisters can cook as well, but when it comes to me and my chicken dressing, I usually put all my sisters out of business. My sister Bonita cooks a delicious oyster dressing, and my mama loves it.

I will never forget the cranberry sauce and the chitterlings. It was so good; you just wanted more and more. Don't mess around and have some freshly grated coleslaw. Some might say they cannot eat the chitterlings because they are nasty, stinking, and disgusting. Well, there is just no way I can do that, so let me say this if you are from the south and did not eat chitterlings, you knew someone who did eat them. I know they stunk up the house back in the day, but it wasn't the holidays without some chitterlings. Some people call it s**tterlin' (LOL). I remember my Auntie Diane used to sell chitlin plates on the weekends. You get some hot sauce and mustard and put them on those chitlins. It made you want to get down like James Brown (LOL).

My Life's Greatest Troubles

I also remember Thanksgiving Day over to the grandparents across the street. Mamacile's sister Aunt Meno and her family would come the Wednesday before Thanksgiving and spend the night. Then Aunt Minnie and cousin Junior came sometime earlier, then Cousin Alice and her son Kemper came later too. Aunt Meno would start cooking then cousin Butch and his family would come over and eat with my father and stepmother. Back then, that was the only time I saw my father. Another time was two or three days before Christmas when he would come to Grandma's house, and my brother, sister, and cousin would go to Mamacile's house. Then Daddy would take us to his job at Lockheed Martin in Marietta, where they had Christmas presents for the employees' children with Santa Claus in one of the warehouses. We got toys and a Christmas stocking with candy and fruit.

My father, Mr. Harold Lewis Smith, was born on November 23, 1929, and graduated from Booker T. Washington high school. He then attended Morris Brown college and then went into the US Army. He worked at Lockheed for 39 years.

I can also write a book on my mother, Mrs. Helen Louise Glass Smith, and title it "That's my Mama" because of who she was and how great she was. Filled with excellence, my mother was a spirit-led woman of God and loved God faithfully with all her heart, spirit, and soul. My mother was also a praying woman. It calls for some praying and calling on God to help her care for her family, whom she loved equally. I often heard her calling on the Lord's name: "Lord have mercy." I'm sure many days and nights, her pillow was wet with tears as she tried to take care of eight children at home. Her love was no different from one to another. My mother loved everybody even if she did not know you like that (that's my mama).

CHAPTER 3

I can remember one Christmas when I was a teenager, and I got a BB gun. I guess, like most kids, I couldn't sleep because I was excited and eager, I just couldn't and wouldn't wait, so me and my brother and I got up and sneaked into the living room early in the morning, and we started playing with our toys under the Christmas tree. I got a daisy BB gun, and well, I got in trouble with that BB gun later on in the summer. During the summer, my cousin Shawna, Uncle Bubba, and Aunt Marie lived next door. Her Auntie Marie Simpson (Big Marie) adopted two kids, Chip and Buck. They would come over sometimes to spend the summer with Auntie Marie while they were out for the summer.

We had fun as kids playing baseball and basketball. We made hot rod cars out of wood and bicycle tires or skate wheels; you name it, we did it. I remember walking up to the elementary school on Macedonia street to play baseball on the field. We took our hot rod cars and raced them down the hills. We would also shoot my BB gun. We set up cans, and Chip, Byeboo, Buck, and I would take turns to see who could hit the most cans. We had so much fun until the trouble with Mr. Wilson, the neighbor. Mr. Wilson, who lived on the other side of my house.

My Life's Greatest Troubles

Remember, we were all shooting my BB gun. I used to keep the BB gun lying around, and Buck used it and accidentally shot out Mr. Wilson's window. Mr. Wilson knew it was my BB gun. Because he did not care for me, he reported that we were in my backyard playing baseball. We threw the baseball against the side of my house, and it went over the fence onto Mr. Wilson's yard. He was outside cleaning and raking his yard when he saw the baseball, so he got the ball and brought it to the fence; keep in mind I still had the baseball bat in my hand. Mr. Wilson says, "here is your baseball," so I go over to him at the fence to take the ball from him, and he grabs and touches me inappropriately.

He approached me wrong and threw the baseball back over the fence. I thought Mr. Wilson would hand the baseball to me, but he did a bad thing, and I swung the baseball bat at him. I don't think it hit him, but he went downtown to the Fulton County Juvenile Court and filed a claim against me, so my mother and I had to go to Juvenile Court. Mr. Wilson told the court that I shot out his window with a BB gun and hit him with the baseball bat. The court put me on probation for a terroristic threat and aggravated assault. Mr. Wilson lied to the court. I was only fifteen and still in high school. My probation officer would come to the school every Friday to make sure I reported to school and class. My probation officer's name was Mr. Gildan.

My Life's Greatest Troubles

Mama bought many cars throughout the years. She bought a 1975 blue 4-door white vinyl top Oldsmobile cutlass supreme. It was clean! This was in 1979. In 1981, this became my very first car. Mama allowed me to start driving after I could go to the Farmer's Market in Forest Park and then to the Georgia Department of Driver Services when I turned sixteen to get my license. At this time, I am attending Walter F. George High School and reporting to my probation officer Mr. Gildan on Fridays so he could be sure that I was keeping the terms of my probation and going to all my classes as required.

I have family moving in and moving out from the Canyon Creek Apartments. My older sister Bonita (Neet) and her husband, Jerry, called (Gip), have lived on Conley Road in the Canyon Creek Apartments in Atlanta since 1975, and are about to move into their new house. This was the early summer of 1980, maybe July. My brother Anthony, we called him (Andy), and Cousin Bernard just moved into the Canyon Creek Apartments together, so they are in the same apartment as Uncle Barry and auntie Mary-Anne who moved into their new house.

My older brother who we call (Greg) and his wife Deborah, who we call (Dee) have moved out as well. I have a sister, Phyllis, who we call (Phil) who moved into the apartment complex in August of 1980. Two other family members have also moved out, and two more moved in. I am still checking on the grandparents who live across the street from me to make sure that Mamacile is ok because she is dealing with Alzheimer's disease. I also check on them after school. Grandaddy Rubin is still moving around a little.

My sister Phil works for Pet Bakery on Grant Street in Atlanta. This is the same place where my mother worked for years, but Phil needed a babysitter, so she asked me to watch her two kids while she went to work in the evening from 5:00 pm to 1:00 am. She agreed to pay me on Thursdays to look after my niece Shyuda (Shy) and nephew Zarkeias (Zark). I am now at the Canyon Creek Apartments, where I get dropped off at my sister's apartment to babysit.

She lives on the front side of an upstairs unit with a balcony that gives a great view. One day when I went there to watch the kids, I noticed a chick downstairs underneath my sister's unit who was staring at me with a smile, so I started looking at her

My Life's Greatest Troubles

with a smile too. I noticed this boy coming in and going out of the apartment where she was, and I thought I knew him, but I did not say anything to him. He kept looking at me, too, and I knew his name was Ken from elementary or middle school.

I don't know if I spoke first to the beautiful fine female with thick eyebrows and chocolate skin. She said something to me, so it was on and popping. Keep in mind I am only 16, but her name is Diana, and she is out of school because she graduated from C.L. Harper High School in Atlanta and is about to go to college at Albany State College in Albany, GA. Diana told me that he was her brother and that he knew me. Oh, I was right about the boy Ken.

While I was babysitting my niece and nephew, and Phil would go to work, Diana would come upstairs to my sister's apartment. She had a stereo system, and I used to blast it when Diana and I would listen to music. Diana and I loved to listen to music. Some of the music we listened to was Teddy Pendergrass "Love TKO" and "Turn Off The Lights." Then we would listen to Teddy and Stephanie Mill's song, "Feel the Fire." Lord have mercy... if we wanted to keep it slow, it had to be some Rick James and Tina Marie singing "Fire and Desire," and then there was Bobby Womack's "If You Think You're Lonely Now." Still keeping it slow with Diana Ross and Lionel Richie's singing "Endless Love," it was on and popping.

My Life's Greatest Troubles

When we were ready for the upbeat music, it had to be the Gap Band with "Burn Rubber on Me" (Why You Wanna Hurt Me) or Yarbrough and Peoples's "Don't Stop The Music." I know you thought I forgot about Michael Jackson's Don't Stop Til You Get Enough." I can go on and on from back in the '80s when real music was played, music that had feelings and real meaning. When we wanted to hear rap without all the cursing and name-calling, it had to be some Sugar Hill Gang with Rapper's Delight or Kurtis Blow singing "The Breaks."

Those were the days when Diana and I were in a relationship, so we would walk up the street to the Waffle House. We would cut through the apartments and come out on the hill. Our usual was a cheeseburger and hash brown or a patty melt plate. We had fun walking to the store to play the arcade games like Pac-Man, Battlezone, Centipede, King and Balloon, Phoenix, and Donkey Kong.

I was in love with Diana. Diana had four brothers. Her brother John and I would hang out with another friend named Roderick, who lived across the hall, upstairs from my sister Phil. We would break into the apartment's washhouse to steal the coins from the washer and dryers. It was easy because the washhouse was never locked. We would use the money to buy beer or weed. We thought that was a lot of fun. Diana was getting ready to go off to college. When she left, it broke my heart. I thought I was the

My Life's Greatest Troubles

man. I was a "bad boy," and nobody could tell me anything. Vee (me) has a college girlfriend at sixteen. My baby Diana was gone, but we decided to write to each other and that I would send her money.

Since my girl was away at college, me and my brothers Andy, Byeboo, my cousin Bernard, friends Gerald Davis, Teno, Big June, Cris Coy, Matthew Gregory, Stanley, Rodney, Shag, Ray, and a few more, started attending the weekend parties at the Canyon Creek Clubhouse. This was in the Fall of 1980. The Clubhouse didn't open some Saturday nights, so we would hang out. On this particular Saturday, I visited my brother Andy and cousin Bernard who would have a get together with family and friends. Keep in mind that I am still on probation but have a good time playing cards, smoking, drinking, and listening to music.

I used to carry a purple crown royal bag which was popular back then and good for carrying whatever you wanted. In my bag, I carried my cologne, money, 1.5 Job rolling papers, and a box cutter. During this time, Wayne Williams was "supposedly" kidnapping and killing young black boys. I really don't think he killed all those black kids.

    While outside at my brother Andy's apartment, I see Cassandra, one of my schoolmates, and her little sister. This young guy named Malik who went to my school and also lived in the apartments was there too. I stopped to talk to Cassandra and her sister who were standing on the balcony. Malik and l were standing on the stairs next to the balcony and I noticed the bottle of beer in his hand. Malik started talking trash about what he was going to do to me. I guess he was getting upset because I was talking to Cassandra and her sister. I kept talking to Cassandra so Malik got up in my face. Now, Malik was a big boy and I didn't like him in my face so I swung. I hit him in the face but it did not faze him. Malik swung and hit my back. His hit spun me around, and I saw stars.

My Life's Greatest Troubles

**Canyon Creek Apartments-
Cassandra's apartment is bottom right.**

I had never been hit that hard. I hit him again, but harder this time, and he broke his beer bottle. He kept coming at me, and before I knew it, I reached into my pocket, pulled out my box cutter, and cut his arm. Blood was everywhere, so I ran into my brother Andy's apartment. Malik followed with his older brother, who was mad and wanted to fight me for cutting Malik. My friend Gerald went to the door and told Malik's brother that nothing would go down in the apartment. He said that it was over, and he closed the door. Gerald then said, "Vee, you know you in trouble now, you cut that boy open and he gone to the hospital!" I asked him why I was in trouble since Malik started with me first. He said, "Vee, first of all, you on probation and you have violated it." He told me to go home and chill out because the police were going to come to my house.

My Life's Greatest Troubles

I went home and told my mother what happened. This happened on Saturday night, it was now Sunday and so far, there was no call and it seemed like everything was good. There was not even a call from my probation officer so I was feeling a little scared. When Monday morning came, the phone rang and it was Mr. Gildan my probation officer talking to my mother who I heard say "okay."

Mama told me I had to go downtown and turn myself in to the Juvenile Authorities. She said it was better for the judge to see that I had turned myself in than to have the police come to arrest me. I told mama I was not going to do that because I didn't do anything wrong, I was just defending myself. I was crying, mama was crying but she still said I had to go. I asked her how long I had to stay but mama didn't know, but we both hoped it wouldn't be for long. I just kept saying it was not my fault.

My mama walked over to Uncle Bubba and Aunt Marie's house and told them what happened. Uncle Bubba came over and talked with me and told me I would be alright and no one would bother me. He told me to hold my head up and asked me where was my faith? I didn't know what to expect as Uncle Bubba drove mama and me down to the Juvenile Court. I was very nervous because I had never been locked up before or even been away from home for that matter.

My Life's Greatest Troubles

After I was processed in, they told me I had to change into a uniform then the Commander-in-Chief laid out the rules and regulations. He said welcome, meet the staff and lights out at 9:00 p.m. I did not sleep at all the first night because I had court the next morning and I kept wondering if I was going home or not. I was in this small room with a hard mattress, hard pillow, two sheets and a blanket with no toilet. Did I mention that the bed was a hard silvery-grey metal frame? If you needed to use the toilet you had to holler out to the commander what your cell number and say "p72 have to use the restroom sir" and wait for the guard to let you out. If you forget to say "sir" they would ignore you and laugh.

The next day in court, I plead guilty to probation violation and they gave me sixty days. I plead guilty because I thought they would let me go home. We showered every evening, four at one time in the stall for 10 minutes each. This time is also for brushing your teeth then watching TV for one hour before lights out at 9pm. Nevertheless, it was sixty days so I had to deal with it because I made a choice and choices have consequences whether good or bad. God is still good even when we are not.

I was able to see my mom on Sundays when visitors were allowed. When she would come to visit me, she would stop by McDonald's and bring me a big-mac, large fries, and a milkshake. I am thankful for my mama, she was the best. I was always glad to see her when she came, but when it was time for her to leave, I was sad but she would tell me "Vernon you are going to be home sooner than you think." "Keep the faith, hold your head up and I love you." I told her I loved her too before she left.

Part of my probation, per Judge Powell, I had to go to school and meet all of the requirements which meant not getting into trouble while in the Detention Center. I had a choice whether to reap the consequences or earn the rewards? The reward for being good was that there was a cookout on Fridays.

Life is made up of decisions and choices. When you better yourself and not get lost or caught up in the world of despair. My mama was my only support and you have to have support. When I had troubles that I created, my mama was there for me, even when the person who had the capability to ruin me quicker than anybody was right inside of me.

Thanks be to God; my time was up in Juvenile Detention and I was happy to be out and glad to see everybody. I still had to see my probation officer Mr. Gildan but I only had a few months left to get off probation.

CHAPTER 4

I couldn't wait to see my grandparents like I always did after school. As soon as I got home, I went across the street to Mamacile and Daddy Rubin's and since she does not lock her back door I walked right in and greeted her. Mamacile said she was glad to see me and that she missed me. She said Daddy Rubin was waiting to see me in his tool house. I told her I missed them too and before I could get to the tool house, Daddy Rubin hollered out to me saying he was glad I was home. I sat and talked to him for a minute before going back into the house where Mamacile was watching TV.

About an hour or so later Mamacile told me she wanted to go home so I tried to tell her she was home but her Alzheimer's was getting worse. She kept saying she wanted to go home even though I knew she was home. I knew I had to be patient with her. She started saying she wanted to go back home. At first I thought at first that she was playing with me because I didn't know what to think because she was home in the house she and grandad built from the ground up. Sometimes she said she "did not want to be in this gambling den". I said ok, then we would sit in grandad's bedroom watching the TV and she seemed alright.

My Life's Greatest Troubles

Mamacile first started showing signs of Alzheimer's in 1978. When Mamacile first told me she wanted to go home it did not bother me because I did not know what she was saying but when she said it the second and third time it scared me a little because I was still thinking that she was playing with me. I kept telling her she was home and she kept telling me that she was not crazy. I did not know what was happening to her but I kept telling her that I knew she was not crazy.

Mamacile had a lot of good days and some bad ones too. There would be days when she was herself but over a period of time the disease gained the advantage over her. On one of her bad days, she said she wanted to go home again when I got in the house. This particular day she was insistent and this time she had two bags and the telephone. She had even unplugged the TV. She said, "we are going home" so I told her I would help her. I was trying to see how far this would go so. I told her to leave the TV because we were walking but she insisted and said she was not leaving her TV, so I told her I would walk back to get the TV and she agreed. I told her to lead the way and I would follow her.

Mamacile started walking behind Macedonia Church which was behind her house. She was alright once we walked around the church and back. I realized that we had to be patient and able to accept and be tolerant of people suffering from this disease

My Life's Greatest Troubles

and not get annoyed. Mamacile and Daddy Rubin were the most patient people I knew. Mamacile's condition was becoming severe.

She would walk away at any time day or night. I remember one day after school I walked over to their house to check on them as usual. Grandaddy Rubin told me that Mamacile took off walking up the street and said that a lady driving on Cleveland Avenue she stopped the car and asked Mamacile if she wanted a ride. Mamacile accepted the ride back to the house. This was really starting to get to me. I was worried about her safety, not just the Alzheimer's disease but the fact that she would get into cars with strangers. I was worried that she could get hit by a car and killed.

I would go to school but I could not stay because my grandparents were on my mind constantly. Grandaddy walked with a cane so when I left school my friend Mark would come with me and I would go to my Grandad's barber shop and sit down

My Life's Greatest Troubles

to watch my grandparents when they did not know we were watching and one day it paid off. Mamacile took off running out of the house down the driveway to the street. I took off behind her, who knew she was that fast and she was strong too. When I caught up to her we just walked and walked until she got tired and then we would walk back to the house. She was good once we got back to the house.

My Aunt Marie would see me in the woods or in the barber shop but she didn't tell anyone. One night when I was about to leave to go home across the street, Mamacile said she was going with me and stated that she did not want to stay in her house because she wanted to go home. I told her she was already home. We had moved her bed into Grandaddy's room so they could be together and he told me to go home because I had school in the morning. She insisted on going with me so Daddy Rubin grabbed her arm and told her to sit down and told me to go. Mamacile dragged him into another room because he held on to her wrist and he did not let go. He hung on but it was funny. He kept saying "Lucille, Lucille stop". They were both strong people. She cried and asked why I was leaving her with that man. It was sad to hear this and it tore me up. I cried because I could not do anything about it. This hurt me so badly, I eventually quit school so I could stay with my grandparents and watch Mamacile when Daddy Rubin would go to the church in Ellenwood to work. I even cooked for them.

My Life's Greatest Troubles

Mamacile was better as long as I was there but her appearance with the disease was increasing. She started cursing me out and calling me names which was a surprise because I did know she knew those kinds of words. I began to really understand her condition. Mamacile's Alzheimer's disease was so aggressive. One day she locked herself in the house. I believe she deliberately locked the door because when Daddy Rubin was knocking and calling her name to open the door Mamacile wouldn't. I even called her name to try to get her to open the door then I walked around the house looking in the windows. I saw her sitting in a chair in Daddy Rubin's bedroom. Mamacile saw me and got up and closed the curtains. Daddy Rubin said, "son, go through the bathroom window and unlock the back door!" "Yes, sir I said," and climbed up in the chair at the bathroom window. I opened the window, and I'm halfway in when Mamacile comes running toward me with a butcher's knife! I jumped backwards out of the window. I thank God, I saw her coming toward me with that knife. Mamacile finally unlocked the door. That was one of her bad days.

My father came and got Mamacile and took her to live with her sister Aunt Minnie on the Westside of Atlanta in Adamsville. This was a predominantly African American neighborhood. Mamacile continued walking away, so my father Harold had to make some difficult decisions. I am sure it was not easy having to decide how to care for his parents.

My Life's Greatest Troubles

It hurt me to see her losing her memory, especially not knowing her own name or her house and even thinking someone was always trying to hurt her when we were trying to help her. It was very frustrating to me and I was angry at times because I could not do anything about the situation. I think the hardest part was feeling like a dagger was in my heart and soul when she would cry. It caused me to get very emotional. My father, Uncle Colvin and Daddy Rubin decided that Mamacile would be better off in a Rehabilitation Center so they chose Crestview Health Center. We visited her for years but she did not know who we were. My heart was broken because my beautiful and loving Grandmother, Lucille Colvin Smith Hambrick, (Mamacile), died on June 1, 1988. I truly miss her, Mamacile rest in heaven.

My Life's Greatest Troubles

CHAPTER 5

*I*n early 1981 I had just gotten off probation and was still caring for my grandparents until Mamacile went to live with Aunt Minnie. I got my driver's license when I turned sixteen so I was sometimes able to drive my mother's blue four door white top 1975 Oldsmobile Cutlass Supreme. My girlfriend and first love Diana was still away at college and I was missing her. Her mom, Mrs. Betty had moved out of the Canyon Creek Apartments to Constitution Hill Apartments in SE Atlanta.

My sister Phil had also moved out of the Canyon Creek Apartments back to the Pinetree Apartments in Forest Park, GA. I was still having the parties with my brother Andy and cousin Bernard who still lived at Canyon Creek Apartments. We had good times on those weekends because a lot of our friends hung out with us too. Let me name a few of those friends: Matthew, Stanley, Gregory, Roney, Gerald Davis, Teeno, Big June, Chris and Byeboo. We had a blast playing cards, smoking, drinking, and listening to music. Andy had a bad music system straight from Radio Shack. It had woofers and tweeters and it all sounded good to me.

My brother Byeboo was younger than the rest of the crew but we let him hang out with us at the

My Life's Greatest Troubles

Canyon Creek Clubhouse, which was the party place. I remember when Byeboo and I used to walk to Canyon Creek Apartments from our house on Jonesboro Road, even in the cold...just to get to the party. Sometimes we would stop and get a half pint of Tanqueray London Dry Gin and a six pack of Olde English 800 and a nickel bag of marijuana. By the time we got to the Clubhouse, we were lit up like a Christmas trees. We would be high as a kite. Keep in mind I was sixteen and Byeboo was only fourteen.

Once we got there it was all over because we took over the party. We were dancing with all the girls; they were all over us too. The real party was downstairs and by the time we hit the bottom of the stairs another girl was pulling me to the dance floor. My brother and I loved to dance, don't mess around and have a dance contest! We would often win but Byeboo was really the one who won the contest most of the time. I can also remember him dancing with Donna Fagan and they won many of the dancing contests.

As a female she was no joke and actually they were both better than good. I remember when the Double Dutch bus came out in 1981, Byeboo won a dance contest at the Holiday Inn for the Double Dutch dance. He had the crowd moving whenever he took the dance floor. We had a lot of fun at those weekend parties from Southeast Atlanta to Forest Park. Byeboo and I went to all of the parties no matter where they were. Even when I didn't drive mama's car, we found a way there for sure.

Whenever Byeboo and I would step out to the clubs, heads would turn. One night we came into the party with white Devo glasses and fresh haircuts that our sister Neet gave us. We had on brand new pairs of Levi jeans from Charlie Trading Post on McDonough Blvd. in Atlanta near the Atlanta Zoo and a new pair of Nike dark blue swoosh logo emblem which were called vintage tennis sneakers. We also got them from Charlie Trading Post or Walter's downtown Decatur Street. We also had on some baby sized baseball caps. The party was over when we walked through the door, especially when the DJ played the number one song of 1981 by Afrika Bambaataa and the Soulsonic Force "Planet Rock."

Byeboo and I would rock the party nonstop as The Sugar Hill Gang Apache (Jump In), Let's Dance Make Your Body Move, Grandmaster Flash, Treacherous Three and many more songs that we enjoyed dancing to. I will never forget 1981. My brother Andy and cousin Bernard moved out of the Canyon Creek Apartments. Cousin Bernard has already moved out. My brother Andy and his girlfriend Sonya moved to Pinetree Apartments in Forest Park, GA. I got a job working at the Thrift Town Grocery Supermarket bagging groceries for $3.35 an hour. This was near the end of 1981 and although the Clubhouse was still doing parties, just

My Life's Greatest Troubles

about everyone I knew had moved out of Canyon Creek Apartments to the Pinetree Apartments.

    One weekend when my girlfriend Diana was home from college, she called me to come over to her house because she wanted to see me. Even though my brother's Byeboo and Andy and Andy's girlfriend already had plans to go party, all that changed. I told them I wasn't going to the party because I wanted to see my baby Diana. They still wanted to go so I told them I would drop them off and come back to get them after I spent time with Diana. I was driving my mother's car, the blue white-top four door cutlass supreme and it was raining so my Auntie Marie asked for a ride too. I was really hoping they would change their minds about going since it was raining and I was trying to get to see Diana before it got too late.

    After having to wait for everyone to get ready, off we went. I was in a hurry to get to Diana's and before I knew what was happening, we started spinning around in the middle of Conley Road. We were spinning out of control. Everybody in the car was screaming. I believe God stepped in and took control of the situation. He got between me and the steering wheel and I felt the breath of God when He took hold of the steering wheel. He revealed himself through signs and wonders because we went into a big wide field off Conley Road. We were still spinning in the field, all I heard was screaming and hollering. I know it was God that stopped the car from flipping over.

My Life's Greatest Troubles

When we finally stopped, the car was next to a big rock on the driver's side. I couldn't open the door so I had to climb out on the passenger side. Everyone was okay. No one was hurt but it was dark and in 1981, there were no cell phones. God opened my eyes to see that the rock was ironic in an opposite dramatic way to what I expected. This could have been tragic but God showed me that He is the rock. It was black and dark in that field. There was no flashlight and it was raining but He allowed me to see that rock.

Forty years ago, God had a purpose for my life because in 1981, God was the last thing on my mind. Partying over here and over there was what was on my mind. Hanging out with the boys and flirting with girls, even though I had a girlfriend in college, was it for me. I was having fun. I had a girlfriend in college, smoked marijuana (joint, reefer) or (gas or loud) as it's called today. I didn't realize it then but God was with me, even when I was not with God. This rock saved our lives.

I opened my eyes to His manifestation. I saw the unseen God at work among us as the Holy Spirit can be seen, felt or experienced. I must say that rock was a rock in a weary land. The rock of ages was an unfailing source of strength. It was strong enough to stop the car from flipping over. That rock revealed to me my refuge and a strong tower against the opponent. God revealed that His very presences helps in times of trouble, making Himself known in a

My Life's Greatest Troubles

dramatic existence to humans in the world, even today. Without a doubt He is right in the midst of my troubles.

Once we are out of the care, I was trying to see where we could find help. It is still raining and the car is stuck in the field. My brother's girlfriend Sonya's aunt lived nearby so we went to her house to use the telephone. Needless to say, there was no party and no visit to see Diana. My life's greatest troubles" has taught me how not to be in a hurry using excess speed. A friend and neighbor Mr. Shag helped me to pull the car out of the field and I was able to see Diana before she went back to school.

CHAPTER 6

I crushed my relationship with my first love Diana. When she was in college because of my actions. I started hanging out at parties and in the streets and I forgot about my love. Yes, I was very young but I understood who I loved for what I knew love to be. Diana was bright and beautiful and I knew she loved me but I threw it all away for no good reason. Ignored her and refused to communicate with her.

I remember one day when she got out of college, her brother came to my mother's house to find me to let me know that she was in the hospital and wanted me to go see her. For reasons I can't really explain, I never went to see her in the hospital. I regret that, even to this day. There is a gash deep in my heart for the sorrow I feel because I was not there when she needed me the most. I know that no matter what, if it had been me in the hospital, she would have been there. I should have been by her side no matter what was going on in my life.

This was the straw that broke the camel's back and ended our relationship. I understand now that life goes on so Diana went out and started her life. She eventually got married and started a family as did I. I pray to God every day that people who I have wronged will forgive me. Charge it to my head and not my heart, sometimes when I am riding in my car and I hear this song "I Do Love You" by GQ. I remember when it first came out in 1979, then in 1980 that is when I first met Diana and that song played. She will always be in my heart.

It is the end of December 1981 and the owner of Thrift Town Grocery has a brother named Bennie Galanti. He owns Bennie Package store on Jonesboro Road in Atlanta which still exists today. Mr. Galanti had two sons, Ronnie and Irwin. Irwin was the son who hired me and gave me my first job. Charles Odom and Charles Johnson were managers at the store. The owner hosted a Christmas dinner party at the Valley Steak House off Cleveland Avenue for his employees every year. I am certain that this was the last time we had the Christmas party because someone got drunk and crashed the party.

1982, I am still working for Thrift Town and still driving my 1975 four door Cutlass Supreme that my mother gave me after the incident on Conley Road the year before. 1982 started out being one of the coldest winters that I could remember other than in 1973. That was when there was an ice storm for two days in January. There was sleet and freezing rain with more than four inches of ice accumulated on the roads. Power lines were down and over 300,000 people had no electricity. Traffic was at a standstill. I remember it well because it was so cold. I was

My Life's Greatest Troubles

working inside bagging groceries and outside with a cart taking groceries to the customers' cars.

It was January 12, 1982, and it is still the coldest day in my life because the temperature was five degrees below zero which was a record low. My mother and sister (Neet) stopped by the store to pick up a few items. Heavy snow had started falling just before rush hour that Tuesday and every flake stuck to the ground. Many commuters who started home never made it. This powerful storm quickly dumped several inches of snow in Atlanta causing a traffic nightmare. The managers, Irwin and Ronnie closed early around, 3 pm but cars were sliding everywhere and were stuck. I could not drive so I had to leave my car and walk home which was about a mile from my job. I will never ever forget that day because very cold or as my Grandaddy Rubin would say, "it's colder than a well diggers butt."

It's springtime and my brother Byeboo and I are still going out on weekends but not as much. The partying has slowed down at the Canyon Creek Clubhouse so everybody is now hanging out at the Tara Skating Rink on Sunday nights. Man, when Byeboo and I went there one Sunday night, Lolly Dolly and everyone was up in there. It was jam packed. We decided that this was the place to be on Sunday nights. Everyone who partied at the clubhouse are now at the skating rink. Now, Byeboo and I cannot skate but it was all good because we were willing to learn. We were working and going out on the weekends, the weather was great and it is about to be summer. It is May 1982 and my heart is broken by the passing of my Aunt Marie. Rest in heaven until we meet again. I really miss you, love you your nephew.

My mother was still working for Pet Bakery. She was buying a new car so she went to her favorite car lot on Stewart Ave. Mama bought a 1974 Buick Regal. It was baby blue with white leather interior and a white vinyl top. When I saw the car for the first time, I just shook my head because it was one of the sharpest Buick Regal I had ever seen. The color was on point! Mama said when she saw me shaking my head, she thought she messed up but I told her she could not have picked a better car. I told her I was shaking my head because of how she went out and picked out a sharp car like that all by herself. My mama did that doggone thing!

Mama was still driving but not as much since her nerves started getting bad when there were too many cars on the road. She would get me to drive her back and forth to work most of the time. Mama would have me stop and pick up her coworker Mrs. Emma in

My Life's Greatest Troubles

Lakewood because she worked at the Pet Bakery too. It was on and popping now that I had the 74 Regal. I was off weekends so it was time to clean it up. I remember smiling, styling, and profiling as I was riding around listening to the car stereo on 1380 WAOK AM. Yes, it was AM not FM like it is today with V103 or KISS 104 FM.

Back in 1982 WAOK was the station to listen to Rap music and all the Jams like: "Planet Rock", "Soulsonic Force", "The Message" by Grandmaster Flash, "The Furious Five", and "Genus of Love" by the TomTom Club. Even though "Dance to the Drummer's Beat" was a nightclub song from the 70's, it would always move the crowd. We would also hear "Hermon Kelly", "777-9311 by The Time, "You Dropped A Bomb On Me" and "Early In The Morning" by The Gap Band, "Let it Whip" by the Dazz Band and "That Girl" by Stevie Wonder. Who can forget about "Billie Jean", "Beat It" and "Wanna Be Startin Somethin" by Michael Jackson.

When we wanted to slow it down a little bit it had to be "Sexual Healing" by Marvin Gaye, "Get Down On It" by Kool and the Gang, "The Girl is Mine" by Paul McCartney and Michael Jackson, "Love Come Down" by Evelyn "Champagne" King "And I Am Telling You I'm Not Going" by Jennifer Holliday, "It's Gonna Take a Miracle" by Denice Williams, "Mama Use To Say" by Junior, "If You Think You're Lonely Now?" by Bobby Womack, "The Lady In My Life" by

My Life's Greatest Troubles

Michael Jackson and "Cruisin" with Smokey Robinson, "Jump to it" Aretha Franklin, and "Let's Stay Together" by Al Green. Believe me, that was "REAL" music back then and the list goes on and on. I had a good time cruising around town some Saturday's in my mother's 1974 Buick Regal with my brother ByeBoo, my cousin Shawna and her friend DeeDee. We would go to the Sans Souci Club on Peachtree Street. WAOK would broadcast live from the club. Man did we have a time back in the day!

My Life's Greatest Troubles

CHAPTER 7

Byeboo and I would still go out from time to time wherever the party was, but our attention was on skating. Now that we knew where everyone was hanging out on Sunday nights, we needed to find a place to learn how to skate. Sometimes we would go to the Marta Train Station near my sister Neet and practice in the parking lot. My sister and her kids would come too, and we would all be skating in the Marta parking lot. It was a lot of fun with all of us out there together. I will never forget the family night when we would go to the Old Dixie Skating Rink in Forest Park.

It was my sister Bonita (Neet), her husband Jerry (Gip), and their three children, Toderick (Todd), Shekeenia (Keena), Aries, my sister Giselle (Zell), her husband Frederick (Fred), their daughter Sheronica, my brother Byron (Byeboo) and me (Vee). We were falling all over the skating rink floor and having a lot of fun. Byeboo and I were getting our practice on. They played songs like John Mellencamp's "American Fool," Survivor's "Eye of The Tiger," Michael Jackson's "Thriller," "Beat It," and so many more. They did not play the songs we heard at Tara Skating Rink, but it was all good because we were learning.

We were having a ball, so we decided to go to different

My Life's Greatest Troubles

rinks. We would go to Skate Towne on Old National on Wednesday night, and we had some good times. Sometimes we would go to Jellybeans at Greenbrier, it was nice, but their floors were tiled and very slippery. One night, Byeboo, our cousin Sharod, Andrew, and I went to Jellybeans and smoked a joint in the men's restroom. An undercover Fulton County Police officer walked in, and guess who the officer caught with the joint in their hands, yours truly! Sharod went one way, Andrew went another and Byeboo went back out the restroom. The police jacked me up and took me to the skating rink office, where I was frisked as they checked through my pocket and found the bag of marijuana on me. The officer took the bag of marijuana and told me to go home. Lesson learned.

 Byeboo and I would still find somewhere to practice. We just about had it now, so it was skating for us on Sunday nights from 8:00 p.m. to midnight. I worked on Sunday mornings and went skating on Sunday nights. My brother-in-law Frederick (Fred) worked at Holiday Inn on Old Dixie Highway in Forest Park, so he was able to get me a job. I was now working at both ThriftTown and Holiday Inn. At the Holiday Inn, I bussed tables, helped in the kitchen, and did room service for tips. I was a busboy bussing tables, helping in the kitchen, and doing some room service for tips. Since I worked two jobs, it was time to upgrade the sound system and fix the Regal. I sold my Cutlass to a co-worker named Jeff for $850.

My Life's Greatest Troubles

It was time to take the factory radio out of the Regal and install a new stereo. I went to this place called CMC Stereo and Radio Shack. I bought a new JVC cassette player stereo with an Audiovox Amp, 7 band equalizer amplifier with two pioneer 6x9 inch with a 12-inch woofer in the middle of the back window. I also went to the Rainbow Muffler in Forest Park and got some air shocks on the Buick Regal to bring it up a little bit because it was so low in the back. We were ready, so Byeboo and I rode out. Everywhere we went, there were a lot of people hating on the Smith boys. At first, they hated on us on Jonesboro Rd, then they started hating on us in the clubs, and now they were hating at the skating rink. We could tell from the expression on their faces that they hated to see the Smith boys coming.

It was Sunday night, and I had just got off work at the Holiday Inn. I went to the car wash to clean the Regal. As Byeboo and I rode out, we smoked and listened to the JVC hits. We headed out early to Tara Skating Rink to get a good parking spot up front. And there we were, Smith Boys in that pretty 1974 baby blue Buick Regal with the 2-inch white wall tires and custom-made rims booming. So, we pulled up, and I turned up the JVC stereo with my mixtape by Edward J. I just had to do it! Heads were turning and shaking. I saw Tino in his big brown Mercury Marquis with the quarter-inch white walls and 15-inch reverse 10-inch Cragar tru spoke wire wheels. We call them "bones" back in the day (wow). Tino was blasting his Marantz

My Life's Greatest Troubles

radio with that "Planet Rock" by Afrika Bambaataa. Scotty B. was driving his green Thunderbird, which was clean. Gerald Davis was driving his Maverick Pig, his mother's Mustang. Even though we knew them and partied with them, they were still hating on us at the party.

The hating continued even though we were at the skating rink. The Smith Boys were in the house, and so was Lolly Dolly, and everybody from Pool Creek to Decatur. Byeboo and I had been practicing, so it was on. We went up to the rental counter, got our skates, and people were just looking at us with a lot of hate, so yes, we were ready. We waited to hear the jams we liked but noticed someone staring at us. It was our friend Andrea from our party days at the Canyon Creek Clubhouse. She told us that she and her friends usually come to skate. As we talked, the DJ told the ladies to clear the floor because it was men-only skate time. Then he dropped the song (Jive Rhythm Trox-127BPM). Byeboo and I hit the floor running.

It felt good as we floated by everyone. Gerald Davis, Teno, and Pig Scotty B were skating in quadruple. We could see the hate as they passed by, telling us to "give a nigger" a little room. This bald-headed black guy and three other people were also skating in quadruples. He was yelling stuff like, "toot-toot MF" and "F that S!" We later found out that the guy's name was Kojak, and he was one of the baddest skaters I have ever seen on the skate floor. We did not know Kodak or his crew, which we discovered were John, Cater, and Wolf Cat. Every time Kojak and his crew would pass us, Kojak would say "toot toot MF" and his crew would say "F that S.". They would do this every time they would skate by us. It was very funny to us. Kojak and his crew had a very unique skating Style so every time they hit the floor it was fun to watch. They will be known throughout the skating rinks. Byeboo and I were having a good time. There were a lot of females up in there so we knew that we would be going back.

     One of Andrea's friends kept staring at me and my brother, I can't remember who spoke first but her name was YuRhonda and she became my girlfriend. YuRhonda was fifteen when we met. She lived in Jonesboro in the Key Stone Apartments. We would talk on the phone for hours. I was crazy about this skinny little black berry girl from Jonesboro. I remember the first time I started going to visit her. Her mother, Mrs. Barnes, wasn't fond of me dating her daughter at first but YuRhonda 's brother Dennis assured her mom that I was a good guy.

     The first time Mrs. Barnes allowed me to come into the apartment, I must say I was l little scared. I never went inside before, YuRhonda would always come out. It was cool though because Mrs. Barnes had cable tv. Cable TV had just come out so it was very popular. I will never forget the first time we watched

My Life's Greatest Troubles

the movie Poltergeist together. We liked hanging out. We would go to the movies in Jonesboro, the game room and sometimes we would go shopping at Southlake Mall in Morrow. I would even take her to get her hair done on Cleveland Ave. The funny thing is that hair salon is still there, forty years later.

    YuRhonda wore a Jheri Curl back then. The Jheri Curl is a permanent wave hairstyle that was very popular among African American's during the 1980's and 90's. It gave the wearer a glossy, loosely curled look. It was invented by hairdresser Jheri Redding and the style looked good on YuRhonda. I would also take YuRhonda to school. She went to Jonesboro High School in Jonesboro where she was very active in sports. Sometimes when I went to pick her up in my 1974 Buick Regal with my JVC stereo blasting, she would be smiling as soon as she saw me coming. I even met some friends, both black and white and we used to go out and eat, just doing what young teenagers did. Every Sunday night my brother ByeBoo and I would head over to the Keystone Apartments after I got off work from the Holiday Inn. At that time ByeBoo was also talking to a girl that lived in Keystone named Loretta. We would pick them up on our way to Tara Skating Rink.

    Sometimes we would stop by my sister Zell and her husband Fred's apartment at Carriage House. We would stop by and smoke a little before we went skating. We would be "right" by the time we got to the

My Life's Greatest Troubles

skating rink and ByeBoo and I would be ready to run and glide with our smooth continuous movement. Believe me, we were higher than a kite. After leaving the skating rink we would go hang out at Krystal's on Hwy 85 in Riverdale. Some people went there to get something to eat while others went there to co-mingle. Many wanted to show off their cars and their sound systems.

     All the hanging out I was doing is pretty much what ended my relationship with YuRhonda. I will admit that it was all because of me. When you are young you are going to make mistakes and bad decisions. You think you have it going on and all that's on your mind is having a good time. Back then, I thought when you met a girl, it was common to get 'em, slit 'em, hit 'em, quit 'em and move on. There is another saying, "young, dumb and full of cum!" Make no mistake, this is not just true for the young but a lot of older people who make bad decisions and make choices that hurt. These decisions can also make us wiser.

CHAPTER 8

*M*istakes are about growth and change because it comes from within and a desire to change. At some point, we all have to grow up. If we continue to do what we have always done, we will continue to get what we always get. Life is a lesson that must be studied every day because every day brings about a new challenge. We must also be careful how we treat people because we really don't know the significance we will play in a person's life. A simple apology when you know you have wronged someone is vital in building or restoring a relationship.

If you have done something wrong to a person and you have not apologized, I don't even care if it has been years ago, you need to do your best to make it right. Sometimes people stop speaking to you and you may not even know why but you should still ask the person what happened. If you know you have done wrong and still haven't apologized then I believe that there is something wrong in your heart. When I pray, I ask God to forgive me if something has been said or done unknowingly that was offensive, Lord please forgive me. If the persons or person reminds you or ask you a simple question of what happened, and you can't give a simple answer, listen...you owe them an apology. I have heard people say they ask God to forgive them of the situation and after he forgives

My Life's Greatest Troubles

them, they don't have to say anything to the person they have offended. They feel that going to God in prayer is enough. Now asking God for forgiveness is the right thing to do, however, we also have to man up to our responsibilities. The golden rule was proclaimed by Jesus of Nazareth, "do unto others as you would have them do unto you." In other words, why not treat them with respect and dignity, this is a two-way street, regardless of what you think or feel!

For example: Remember my girlfriend YuRhonda? Remember I told you our relationship ended because of me? Now YuRhonda was a good person, she was very nice. It has been 40 years since YuRhonda and I met and started dating. I had not seen her in over 30 years. In 2016, I created a Facebook account, (I thank God for the technology). While on Facebook, a message pops up on messenger asking me if I was Vernon Smith from Atlanta, that lived on Jonesboro Road back in the day. I messaged back yes this is Vernon Smith from back in the day. It was YuRhonda.

We begin to message each other back and forth and then she asked me if she could call me on the phone. I understood clearly that she was married and I respect that. I said yes, as long as it was not going to be a problem with her husband. YuRhonda called me and we were glad to hear from each other. We laughed and talked about the good old days for a while. We were still talking about the fun times we had when

My Life's Greatest Troubles

YuRhonda, out of nowhere, ask me a question. She asked me "why did you leave me for Rita?" It felt like she hit me with a brick.

All of the laughing stopped. I had to pause for a moment because I didn't have an answer. I had never really thought about it. She said, "Vernon, I thought everything was good with us." She said what hurt her the most is that I never said anything. I just walked away and never said why. She said that it took her years to get over that because the way I treated her, was so good. She couldn't understand what happened. She remembered all the times I would take her to school and pick her up and take her shopping and how we would hang out at the movies and the skating rink. This really hurt my heart. Even while she was saying all this, I felt something prick my heart. I never knew how she felt until she asked me that simple question.

One thing I know is that God will convict your heart if Christ is within you. It's not in me to do people wrong. If I'm wrong, I have to apologize, so that's just what I did. Apologizing to YuRhonda on the phone was not enough. God kept dealing with me in my heart over the situation. I text her and ask if I could meet her somewhere and if she could bring her husband. I just needed to apologize face to face. I invited them to dinner at TGI Friday on Camp Creek parkway. We had dinner and I apologize to her in person. I'm happy to say we are still good friends today. God would not allow me to go on until I made it right with her. Real men steps are ordered by God. You have to do what's right in your heart because God speaks through thoughts and feelings Amen?

CHAPTER 9

*I*t's 1983, a brand-new year and I'm still going to the Tara skating rink in Riverdale on Sunday nights. Me and ByeBoo are still hanging out as usual. I'm driving my baby blue Buick Regal and blasting my JVC stereo through the neighborhood listening to some King Edward J, the Godfather of Atlanta mixtapes. I'm playing some Whodini, Grandmaster Flash, Afrika Bambaatoa and more from the one mixed cassette tape. King Edward J was the man with the tapes when it came to music back in the '80s. Man, I can remember driving to Decatur on Fayetteville Rd to Edward J shop across from East Hampton Apartments, to buy some hot mix jams.

We had a blast in the past in Decatur "where it's greater!" I'm driving and riding around in the neighborhood, booming my JVC stereo and I decided to stop by our good friend Gerald Davis house. He lived with his mother on Villa Circle in the Poole Creek area. I wanted to talk at him about detailing my Regal. Just then, this petite brown skinned pretty girl came outside. The music was loud so I assumed it got her attention. She lived across the street from Gerald. Gerald was picking with her, calling her "bones!" I was watching her. I knew she wasn't taking his teasing to heart because she was smiling. She was looking at me

My Life's Greatest Troubles

as I was looking at her and she kept that smile on her face. That smile caught my eyes. Her eyes were captivatingly beautiful with those glossy lips.... you are talking about a young tenderoni. The funny thing was, we never said a word to each other that day.

A week or two later, Gerald's Nephew Kion whom we call Rabbit, would come to the skating rink with his uncle. Now Gerald and Rabbit were two of the best skaters I know. But, hold up a minute, I wasn't so bad myself...(lol). Seriously, I was no joke on those skates, believe it! I wish cell phones were available back then, I could have captured some golden moments of those good old days on the skating floor.

Kion called me at home and told me that shorty wanted to holler at me. I asked him who? He said Rita and I jokingly said, "who me?" Rabbit said "yeah, yeah you!" I laughed and I told him to give her my number. I don't remember who called first but I think it was Rita because Rabbit never gave me her number. However, it happened, we started talking to each other. She wanted to see me and I wanted to see her but before we could, she had to get permission from your mother. Rita's mother, Mrs. Diane said yes, I could see Rita but only if I would bring her a six pack of Old English Beer. I said to myself, "she ain't said nothing but a word!" Of course, I said yes! I really wanted to see Rita so I went to Benny's Package store on Jonesboro and bought her mother the 16oz tall

My Life's Greatest Troubles

cans of Old English just to see her. I have the beer and I am driving over to meet Rita and her mother, Mrs. Diane for the very first time. Everything is good when I get there but the question never came up about how old I was. I didn't even ask Rita how old she was but I did ask her if she was hungry.

When she said yes, I asked her what she wanted and she said Burger King. I told her to ask her mother if she could ride with me to Burger King and her mom said yes, as long as I took care of her daughter. "I got her, Mrs. Diane" I said. Then Rita and I drove off to Burger king where she ordered the Whaler Fish sandwich combo with fries and a drink. The Whaler made a return at Burger King in 1983 and it was very popular. She got her food and we were riding around in the neighborhood and listening to music while she ate. We rode through Blair Village, Poole Creek and drove through the projects, Gilbert Gardens Apartments on Gilbert Road. They were called the Rabbit box and the Squirrel Box, it was two sets of apartments but they were all together on Gilbert Road, SE Atlanta.

We were riding in my baby blue Buick Regal through the Squirrel Box which was on the top of the hill from the Rabbit Box with my JVC stereo blasting. I could hear people on the sidewalk saying, "who is that?" I heard someone say, Rita. Rita's best friend Sharon (shell), lived in the Squirrel Box and was yelling out to Rita. She asked me to stop so I stopped

My Life's Greatest Troubles

so they could talk. I sat there while they talked. After a few minutes we drove back to her mother's house, talked for a while, then I went home because I had to work the next day.

Even though I was still working two jobs, Thrift Town Supermarket and Holiday Inn, Rita and I talked on the phone a lot. Sometimes I would stop by her mother's house after work on the weekends. Rita went to Walter F. George High School so I would take her to school and go back to pick her up on my off days. I would go over to see Rita on the weekends and we would walk up to Blair Village Elementary school which was up the street from where she lived. When we were talking, I would look into her eyes which seemed to hypnotize me. Her lips were always glossy and smooth when we kissed so sweetly (just the thought makes me shake my head).

We used to walk to the school just to kiss, not a smack but a real French kiss using our tongues. Man, what you say... tongue all the way down the throat! (lol) and Rita kept it fresh with her double mint gum. One day I was off work and went to pick up Rita from school. I parked and was playing my music while I was waiting for her to come out. Rita's friend Shell walked over to the car and told me that Rita would be out soon. She said, "what's up?" I said "nothing much" then Shell opened my car door and got in the passenger seat.

My Life's Greatest Troubles

I didn't have a problem with that because she was Rita's friend but when Rita came out and saw Shell sitting in the car she snapped on her friend. She opened the door and told Shell to get the hell out of her man's car and told her friend she does not play that. My eyes got really big. I did not know she had all that in her because she was so small. Rita was pissed off! I was used to seeing this sweet and quiet, very beautiful eyes of the beholder. Rita's eyes reminded me of Japanese eyes that tend to slant upward. I started calling Rita my baby Tinkernese.

It was time to upgrade on the Buick Regal so I went to Moreland Ave to buy some new wheels. It's the weekend and I have my brand-new rims and tires so we are going skating as usual and Baby Blue Regal is clean. It's Sunday night and guess who I'm taking skating with me? Yes, my new girlfriend Rita. We have to get there early so I can park upfront by the entry door. I already knew Tino from Poole Creek in his big Mercury Marquis, Captain Fat from Decatur in his Dodge Polara 4 door, Dwight from Decatur in his 4-door Ford LTD would all be there. Everybody was trying to get there early for the car show and get the closest parking spot. Yours truly Vee, was going to be up in there in the 1974 baby blue Buick Regal with her new rims and wheels and my foxy lady, Rita in the front seat.

I pulled up to the front of the skating rink blasting the JVC with some Run DMC, "It's Like That

My Life's Greatest Troubles

and That's The Way It Is," "Sucker M.C. and some Whodini, "The Haunted House Rock." I was starting to show off and everybody starts to hate when I elevate. I was a bad man but it's all in good fun.

It's 1984 and my girlfriend's mother Mrs. Diane moved from Villa Circle in Blair Village to the Flamingo Apartments on Cleveland Ave with her friend Mr. Henry who is called (Bear). Rita and I are still together and I still go see her, but now on Cleveland Ave. I am no longer working at the Holiday Inn or Thrift Town Supermarket. I was hired as a United Food and Commercial worker on Old National Highway in College Park through Mr. Curtis William, we call him (Mickey). I was now working at the Cub Food on Jimmy Carter Blvd. in Norcross, GA. It was a nine to five but the traffic was hectic. I was still hanging out at the skate club but not as much on the weekend. All I really did was work and hang out with Rita.

Rita's mother was constantly moving. She moved again, but this time to the Greenwood Apartments on Springdale Rd, in East Point. One summer weekend, I went to visit Mrs. Diane. Her friend Bear invited me to go with them to see a movie. We went to the National Triple Theatre on Old National Hwy in College Park. The movie we went to see was Richard Pryor in Brewster's Millions.

Summer of 1985 was a blast for us! I'm still

My Life's Greatest Troubles

working for the United Food and Commercial by this time. My brother Byeboo is working there too, but we still hang out on weekends. My girl Rita is now working after school at Long John Silver. Sometimes Rita would come over to my mother's house on Jonesboro Road. Rita's mom moved again, this time to the Lakewood Apartments off Pryor Road in Atlanta.

It is around December and very cold. Rita is now working for Yasin Seafood on Stewart Avenue with one of her friends from school named Vanessa. Vanessa lives on Springdale Rd in East Point and Rita would sometimes ask me to take her home. Mrs. Diane's friend Bear also lives in the Lakewood Apartments. When I say it was cold in those apartments, it was COLD! I had to go home and ask my mother if I could use her electric heater. My mother never minded helping anybody if she could because she had a pure heart and I take after my mother. She said yes to borrowing the heaters so, I took them over to their apartment to make sure they were warm.

One night, I decided to wait at Rita's house until it was time for me to pick her up from work. As I sat on the sofa watching Knots Landing and Dallas on TV, I hear, BOOM, BOOM, BOOM! I was so scared, I hit the floor. Next thing I know, Mr. Bear has a stick in his hand hitting the windows busting them out. It was

My Life's Greatest Troubles

so loud, it sounded like someone was shooting. I didn't know what was going on but Mrs. Diane was sitting there smiling looking at me on the floor. She was very calm and she seemed like she was cool with what Bear was doing. I felt so embarrassed because here I am on this woman's floor trying to hide while she is looking cool, calm and collected. Mrs. Diane knew what Bear was going to do because she had gone to his apartment and busted out all his windows first. Man, I got out of there fast. I ended up going to Rita's job and waiting for her to get off work.

It's January 28, 1986, and it's cold outside. Rita and her mom are still living in Lakewood Apartments. I will never forget the fatal accident that happened. It was just before noon; I was at Rita's house watching television. Seconds into the flight, the Space Shuttle Challenger broke apart, killing all seven crew members aboard. This disaster was so sad it messed me up. Sometimes I would spend the night with Rita. Mrs. Diane and Bear were back together. She would often stay at Bear's apartment. When I know Rita's mom was gone and would not be coming home, what do you think I was thinking? Yes, I was staying overnight with my girlfriend. While her mother is not there, it's trouble!

My sister Neet got hired at United Food and Commercial Worker at the Cub Food in Norcross with ByeBoo and me. When none of us showed up for work, we were all fired on Super Bowl Sunday so we

My Life's Greatest Troubles

had to start working on the weekend under new management. Curtis (Mickey) called us to come back to work that next Wednesday. This is why I was able to see the Space Shuttle Challenger disaster, otherwise I would have been at work. We got our jobs back but the supervisor was prejudiced and did not care for us. She tried to discredit us. She knew we always worked together so she was trying to split us up. In the spring of 1986, the company opened new job sites on the southside of Atlanta. They opened one on Jonesboro Rd in Forest Park and the other one on Tara Blvd in Jonesboro. My brother and I decided to go to the Forest Park site but Neet went back to Norcross at Cub Foods because she did not like the southside.

By this time, Rita is working for United Food and Commercial Worker in Forest Park at Food Giant but she is not feeling well. She is getting dizzy and vomiting every morning. She could not work outside in the heat because it made her sicker. Rita decides to go to the clinic and finds out she is pregnant. Wow, I was going to be a father. I did not know what to say to Mrs. Diane or my mother for that matter. There really was nothing to say because it was what it was. We knew exactly what we were doing from the beginning. Now what I did know was that I really had to get myself together on what to do next, knowing that I was soon going to be a father.

I was still working for United Food and they were sending me to the Food Giant on Tara Blvd. I

My Life's Greatest Troubles

was tired of going from one place to the other, so I quit. Mrs. Diane is moving again. This time to the Richmond Oaks Apartments on Richmond Circle and Sawtell Ave SE Atlanta next to the South View Cemetery on Jonesboro Road. I needed to get up and find a job, especially since I had a child on the way. I bought a newspaper to check out the "want" ads. I see an ad for Hu-Ray Cleaning Company so I called the secretary and she tells me to come in and complete the application for employment.

By the time I got back home, Mr. Raymond (Ray) called and offered me a job. He asked me to meet him at the Ryder Truck line on Jonesboro Road. Once I got there, he showed me around and explained what the job requirements were and asked if I could start the next morning. I thanked the Lord for blessing me and providing for me. Most of all I thanked Him for surrounding me with people who always looked out for me.

My job was to keep the building clean; the breakroom, the restrooms and sweep the docks. This was sweet because I was less than a mile from home and less than a mile from my girlfriend's house too. I told my girl that I had a job with the Hu-Ray Cleaning Company and I wanted us to move in together but she wants me to ask her mother. Mrs. Diane says yes because she knows I want to be with my baby Tinkernese.

My Life's Greatest Troubles

My job is gravy and my girl is a go-getter and she loves to work. She was about six months pregnant when she got a job at McDonald on McDonough Blvd. It was less than a mile from where we lived. We were both trying to prepare for our newborn and a place of our own so we were grinding to make that happen. I tell you that God had a hand on me because I am blessed. I started a new job and changed my hours so I could go into work at 6 or 7 a.m. because Rita had to be to work at 5 a.m. so I drop her off and then go to my job at the Ryder truck line. Whenever I got there before 8 a.m. I had to check in with security before they could let me in the building. One morning as I was talking to the security officer, he told me that his company, Advance Security was hiring.

I took the Marta bus then the train to Midtown and applied for the security job. To get the position I had to take a test. I passed and got the job. It was getting late and I needed to get home as soon as possible. The bus was taking too long so I called my sister-in-law Deborah (Dee) to pick me up and take me to Rita's house. I'm thankful to my sister-in-law for looking out for me. I had my uniforms and my equipment. I was blessed to have had two jobs in the same area, how sweet was that? I would clean for Ryder from 6am until 2pm, go home for about 45 minutes, then I'd go back to Ryder and do security from 3pm until 11pm.

I worked like that for about two months until

My Life's Greatest Troubles

one night the staff supervisor came to Ryder and told me that I could not work for Hu-Ray Cleaning Company and Advanced Security at the same time. He told me it was against policy so I had to decide which job I was going to keep. The security job was good but they only gave me a radio and a flashlight. I remember one night while I was on duty, a man was breaking in the back of a pickup truck and he had a gun on him. I saw him in the "clear" from where I was sitting in my car. I really did NOT see him (if you know what I mean). You can call me the three wise monkeys, see no evil, hear no evil, and speak no evil.

What would I look like confronting this man knowing he had a gun and I only had a walkie talkie and a flashlight? It would not have looked good in the Atlanta Journal Constitution or on the WSBTV breaking news with Mark Winnie or Fox 5 News with Amanda Davis. The news report would have said that a 21-year-old security guard played hero and died for doing what was right. He leaves behind a pregnant girlfriend, a mother, father, sisters, and brother. I said all this to say that sometimes God will allow situations and circumstances in which one finds oneself in a state. I believe that the gun was the state of condition that He allowed me to see to make a wise decision. Of course, I chose Hu-Ray Cleaning. It was an easy choice over a security job any day.

One morning I took my girlfriend to work at McDonalds. She had a 5:30am shift. Sometimes I

My Life's Greatest Troubles

would go to work after I dropped her off but since I wasn't working security anymore, I would go in at 7 or 8am. This particular day, I went back home to the apartment. Rita would always call to let me know she was good and she wanted to make sure I was good as well. We talked every morning, even at work. Even though there were no cell phones, I had a pager so we would call the house phone.

This day was strange because Rita had not called me as she usually did. I was assuming she was busy but was still wondering what was up. I decided that I was not going to go to work until she called me. We never went without talking before we started our workday. After about an hour (it seemed like forever), Rita finally called and she was hysterical. She was very emotional and very upset. Rita told me the McDonalds was robbed and the perpetrator ordered everybody in the freezer. Keep in mind that Rita is pregnant with our child.

Man, when I say I rushed up to McDonalds on two wheels! I went and got my girlfriend! I needed to make sure she was calm so I wasn't working any more that day. I stayed off with her to make sure she and my baby were alright. Rita said the perpetrator had a shotgun that he pointed at her, which must have been terrifying. I knew something had to be wrong because we never went without talking to each other. Thank God no one got killed or hurt.

CHAPTER 10

*W*e were still working trying to save money for our own apartment and for our unborn child. It was the holiday's and the baby was coming soon. We had everything our baby would need: pampers, crib, baby bottles and baby rocker. You name it, we had it. We were ready. Rita was nine months pregnant and it was New Year's Eve. Everybody was celebrating that 1986 had come to an end but guess where Rita and I were? We were at the Grady Memorial Hospital; Rita was in labor! Just after midnight at 1:00 a.m., January 1, 1987, on New Year's Day, we became the proud parents of a baby boy we named, Vernon Torrance Smith, Jr. He is my name sake and I was so happy that everything went well with the delivery. I thanked God it was a brand-new year with a new son on New Year Day January 1, 1987. It was time for a celebration.

After we get home from the hospital, we wanted to thank everyone that came down to the hospital to visit us. We had a "Grady baby", Vernon Jr. and I am proud to say that I am a "Grady baby" too! My mother, Mrs. Helen, came to see us at the hospital but my father Mr. Harold came to the apartment in Richmond Oaks to see his grandson. My father was glad everything went well with the delivery

My Life's Greatest Troubles

and everybody was home.

Mr. Ray called me to check on me and our new son. He asked me if I wanted to clean another freight line three times a week. After telling him yes, he told me to meet him over to the Central Freight line on Moreland Ave. It was basic cleaning and fundamentals which I already knew. He showed me around and said I would be working on Monday's, Wednesday's and Friday's and the job paid bi-monthly. I agreed and said thank you to him. He then told me that our services were no longer needed after that month at the Ryder Truck line on Jonesboro Road because the contract would be up in thirty days. Now I have to find another full-time job.

Wow! "My life's greatest Troubles" has begun! I had a new baby, my full-time job was ending and now my car was acting up. On top of all that, we were also trying to move into our own apartment. I headed to Decatur to my Uncle TC's house to let him check out the car, and you guessed it, my car was barely running because it needed a new engine. We just had a new baby and my full-time contract is also ending at the end of the month. It seemed like everything got complicated all at once but thank God I caught a little break from all the problems.

I had money saved, so I went to the "buy here, pay here" car lot on Stewart Ave and bought a new car. It was better for me to buy a new vehicle than

My Life's Greatest Troubles

replace the engine in my Buick. I found a "new" used car, a 1982 Buick Electra Park Avenue sedan. It had four doors and was champagne colored. It was right and tight. We moved from Rita's mother's place to my mother's house on Jonesboro Road. Vernon Jr. was about 4 months old, and it was April 1987. Rita was looking for a job and found one at Hartsfield Atlanta Airport in May of 1987. Things were looking good. I had a new car, was still working for Hu-Ray cleaning company, and our first apartment came through. Thank God for all of His blessings.

We moved to the Heritage Trace Apartments on Forest Park Road SE Atlanta. Rita and I had been buying furniture on layaway, so we fixed up the apartment. The living room was blue, so I changed the carpet to royal blue, my favorite color, and it was glass and brass in our apartment. I felt blessed that we were both working and had our own place. Sometimes my sister Neet and my mom would keep our son. We started calling Vernon Jr. by his middle name, Torrance.

Rita worked from 3:30pm to 11:00pm at the airport. I was working for Hu-Ray, but I could make my own hours. Everything was great. My brother, Byeboo, is even working with me at Hu-Ray Cleaning. I had multiple jobs. I worked at Carolina Freight and Hu-Ray Cleaning in Conley, Monday thru Friday, and at Forest Park State Farmers Market on the weekends. Sometimes I would strip floors for Hu-Ray Cleaning

My Life's Greatest Troubles

for extra money because they had many jobs throughout Atlanta. They were a great company to work for

One morning I let my brother Byeboo use my car. It was very early, around 4 or 5am. Byeboo got into an accident, flipped over, and totaled the car. I thank God he was not hurt or killed, but now I had no transportation. What was I going to do? I had multiple jobs, so I had to think about how I would get back and forth to work. I called a cab the following day to take me to Carolina Freight on Henrico Road in Conley. Sometimes I would walk three miles to work from Moreland Avenue to Forest Park Road. I took the back roads to our apartment. I was so tired, but I had to do what was necessary to keep all my jobs and take care of my business. God was right there with me because better days were coming. God blessed me because of my efforts, even though I was not thinking about God, He was thinking about me.

Mr. Ray from Hu-Ray Cleaning would come and pick me up for work and drop me off. That was a blessing because he was the owner. I felt that was a favor from God because Mr. Ray did not have to do that for me. He could easily have told me he had to let me go because I couldn't get to work. I counted it all joy when I fell into various trials knowing that the testing of our faith produces patience. Mr. Ray could have given up and hired someone else, but it all worked out for good because of his patience and my

My Life's Greatest Troubles

patience. Mr. Ray saw me as more than just a good worker but also a good person. Mr. Ray is Caucasian and was all in the "hood," coming to pick me up and take me to work. This was back in 1987.

Mr. Ray had no business in the "hood", he could have easily gone in and not come out. He could have been robbed or killed... real talk! One morning, when Mr. Ray came to pick me up, he said he would go and get me a car and finance it. All I needed to do was make the payments on time. My eyes got big! I said, "really?" I told him I would make sure I paid on time, so he financed a 1979 Maroon Malibu Classic 4-door sedan. Look at this, God will provide during the storms of life, even when you are not serving Him. The Lord is a stronghold for the oppressed, and God's perfect timing does two things. It grows your faith when you are forced to wait, and God will provide your every need at the right time. I thank God for providing my need for a car through Mr. Raymond. He told me he had more jobs available, and I told him I was ready. I started a new job cleaning at McMaster-Carr on Fulton Industrial Blvd. in Southwest Atlanta.

CHAPTER 11

*I*t's another year, our son Torrence is one year old, and spring is here. We are not signing another lease at the Heritage Trace Apartments, so we are moving again. It is rough on the Southside of Atlanta, so we are moving in with Rita's grandmother, Mrs. Elaine Jackson, until our apartment is ready. I got another building to clean with Hu-Ray Cleaning at the Wilson Trucking Corp on Moreland Ave, Conley, GA. The Carolina Freight line is moving to a bigger facility. I was heartbroken in early summer when Mamacile died on June 1, 1988. Lucille Colvin Smith Hambrick passed on to be with the Lord. She had been sick for a long time and was in the Crestview Health Rehabilitation Center in Atlanta for years. The funeral was held at the Greater Ephesus Missionary Baptist Church in Atlanta on June 6, 1988. It was directed by Seller Brother Funeral Home. Mamacile is buried in Forest Lawn Memorial Garden in College Park, GA. RIP Grandma Mamacile. You will be missed.

    I was working a lot trying to save money to move again. I had multiple jobs all over the city. Grandaddy Rubin was in the hospital at Emory Crawford Long Hospital in Midtown Atlanta. Daddy Rubin had many health issues and had lost his sight. He died on December 13, 1988, and my heart was broken again. His funeral was held at his church, Zion

My Life's Greatest Troubles

Grove Baptist on Old Toney Road in Ellenwood Ga. He is buried in the Macedonia Cemetery in Forest Park. Grandaddy Rubin knew a lot of things, he was my hero. Thank you, RIP.

    1988 has gone and it's 1989. My mother moved into my grandparents' house at 3265 Jonesboro Road, across the street from where we lived. Our son is now two years old and we are moving from Decatur back to the Southside of Atlanta to Kingston Townhouse Apartments. Rita's mother Mrs. Diane and her brother Alfred Jr moved in with us for a while. Rita has two brothers Alfred Jr. and Roderick who we call (Rod).

    My brother Greg is a minister under the leadership of the Reverend M. Davis at the Greater Ephesus Missionary Baptist Church in Atlanta. Greg was called to pastor the Floyd Chapel Baptist church in Stockbridge. Under their leadership Reverend Greg, Deborah (Dee), me, Rita and our son Vernon joined the Floyd Chapel Baptist Church on 1st Street in Stockbridge. I must say, we were in church but the church was not in us. Nevertheless, I thank God for allowing me to be at church and I must say again I did not know God in my sins but thank God, He knew me. This is why I praise Him even more today because I know Him now.

    Rita's baby brother Roderick (Rod) was a young hustler in the streets. He made money selling

My Life's Greatest Troubles

crack cocaine in Pool Creek area, The Rabbit Box and the Squirrel Box. The apartments were called Gilbert Garden. Rod started in the projects with big bags that he had to break down to dime bags which could be easily sold. He sold his dime bags for ten dollars. They could easily be sold for twenty dollars so you made a ten-dollar profit. Roderick had them "boulders like shoulders and bricks like tricks." Rod had that glass and butter, that "hard-hard." How do I know all that you might be thinking? Well, it's because I've done it. I started getting the break downs from Rod in late 1989.

We were about to move out of Kingston Townhouse to Briarwood Apartments on Hapeville Road, our apartment was on the backside. I remember one cold night our apartment caught fire. We were all there when it happened, I remember waking up from the smoke and fire. Rita was cooking chicken and we both fell asleep. Our son was upstairs in the bedroom sleeping, I was on the couch, and Rita was in the chair. We had only been there for a week or two. After waking up from the smoke I ran upstairs to get our son and we all got out. Thank God no one was hurt.

There were no cell phones at that time so we were waiting for Bell South to come out and install our telephone services. Our neighbor would not even let us use their phone to call the fire department. I did not understand the neighbor. We were new to the neighborhood so I thought at least they would do was

My Life's Greatest Troubles

call 911 for us. Instead, I had to run over to the next set of apartments to my friend Leon's. Thank God I was able to get him to call the fire department. Our apartment was damaged due to the fire but I was so thankful no one got hurt. We ended up having to stay with my mother for a few days until another unit was ready for us.

I was still holding down my job with Hu-Ray Cleaning company. I was the lead man at Carolina Freight Line on Thurman Road. I had a lot of people working under me, including my two brothers, Andy and Byeboo. My friends Mike-Mike, Dexter, Satterwhite, David, and Bruce worked there too. Now, Mr. Ray and I had problems, and I needed to find another job! Mr. Ray started asking too much of me. He had even changed his tone when he talked to me, and it seemed like we did not see eye to eye because he started talking to me disrespectfully. I don't care who you are or what you have. If I respect you, then I want respect in return. Shortly after I left Hu-Ray Cleaning Company, Mr. Ray lost the contract with the Carolina Freight Line, but I'm still doing me...selling crack cocaine.

I found another job with Craig Cleaning Service in the Ansley and Piedmont Avenue area in late 1989. I did a lot of different jobs with Craig Cleaning Service. I cleaned all the Georgia Federal Banks on the south side, East Point, Riverdale, College Park, and the one in the Ansley shopping center. I also cleaned a

My Life's Greatest Troubles

business called Computer World on Jimmy Carter Blvd. in Norcross. I was rolling! Everything was going well. It was the holiday, and I was making money.

I had customers that worked for Service Merchandise, Sears, and Rich's that bought crack from me. They would trade all kinds of retail for some crack cocaine. You name it, I had it. I could get a set of brand-new Michelin or Goodyear tires for the low low. I was the first to get my girlfriend a KitchenAid Mixer, which was about $700 to $1000 back in the 1980s. Christmas of 1989, Rita and I gave everyone in our family gifts. We gave everything from jewelry, electronics, toys, coats, and clothing to home appliances. The Christmas tree was packed at our Briarwood apartment that year.

The New Year has come, it is 1990, and we have just celebrated our son's third birthday. It is time for me to upgrade my 1979 Malibu Classic. I already had some 50-spoke wire wheels with Vogue tires, and sad to say, someone stole my car from my mother's house on Jonesboro Road. Thank God I found my car one night behind a vacant house on Mt. Zion, but it was stripped down. I had to get a new steering column, wheels, and tires, but it was cool because I had the hook-up with one of my customers that worked for Sears in the Westend. I bought a set of 30-spokes, true wire wheels from Hubcap Bob on Jonesboro Road. The Malibu was clean and sharp.

My Life's Greatest Troubles

One night, not long after getting the car back, I remember being asleep upstairs around 3am when I heard my car door open. I told Rita that someone was in my car or trying to get in; I did not have a car alarm on the Malibu then, so I got up and grabbed my pistol. I looked out the window and saw two men sitting in the front seat of my car, one black and one white. I shot about three or four times, and while I was firing, they took off running. I assume they were trying to steal my Malibu. I had to replace the side window that they broke while breaking in. I put a chain around the steering wheel with a lock, but the perpetrators had a padlock cutter with them. They forgot to grab it when they ran away after I shot at them. This all happened in 1990 while we were still living in Briarwood Apartments.

The new year has rolled in, and we celebrated our son Vernon's fourth birthday. We had lived in the Briarwood apartments for a year and were about to move to the Colonial Square Apartments across the street from Kmart on Cleveland Ave. I am no longer working at Craig Cleaning Service on Jimmy Carter Blvd. All the Georgia Federal Banks and the building on Jimmy Carter that I was cleaning were given to another employee because they wanted me to clean in Buckhead. It was a lot more work and not enough pay, plus driving every day in the traffic was a nightmare. I quit the job after working for two days. I had to find another job because we had just moved. I am blessed that I found one. Matthew 7:7 says, Ask, and it shall

My Life's Greatest Troubles

be given to you, seek and you shall find, knock and it shall be opened to you. Ask and keep asking, and it will be given to you. I am talking from the physical. Yes, it is good to name it and claim it, but you have to go and knock on doors physically to find a job.

While working as a groundskeeper for the City of Eastpoint's Parks and Recreation, I was still hustling. Rita worked for Atlanta Gas Light in the cafeteria on Moreland Avenue near Little Five Points. Shortly after we moved into the Colonial Apartments once again, my life's greatest troubles began with my car. The heathens were trying to steal my car again. This time I called 911. The sad part was that the Atlanta Police never showed up.

They didn't come to investigate even after I called them numerous times. The thief ran away after I opened my bedroom window and hollered, "GET AWAY FROM MY CAR BEFORE I SHOOT YOU!" I had to replace another side window on the passenger side again, but I thank God, they could not steal it. It was crazy over there, so we only signed a six-month lease. It was rough. People were always walking around, day and night.

I noticed the landlord, Mrs. B, did not care for us moving into the apartment, and I think I know why. The apartment's policy was to inspect the unit a week after a tenant moved in. When Mrs. B. came, she brought a person who was supposed to be a

My Life's Greatest Troubles

maintenance person to conduct the inspection. However, I knew he was an undercover police officer. He had a pen and pad and was dressed in blue jeans, boots, and a flannel shirt. I knew he was a police officer because I saw him in Zone 3 on the streets of Atlanta in his police car. I played along with it but later found out that someone we knew called the rental office and told the landlord we were selling drugs. They were jealous and actually said to us that they were going to call the rental office. It was cool because you never trap out the place where you lay your head.

Well, the landlord and the so-called maintenance man (undercover police officer) found nothing but a nice and clean apartment. Mrs. B. even said that we had a lovely apartment with nice furniture. Thank you we said (but we were thinking, "yeah, right!"). Our furniture was nice if I must say so myself. Rita and I bought the floor model televisions in each bedroom, the living room set, and the dinette set with bar and stool from Heilig-Meyers and Rhodes furniture company in Hapeville, Ga. Be careful; some people are jealous of you and what you have. You can't invite everybody into your home, and that's a fact.

In the mid-'80s, the only way to contact anyone outside of a home phone was through a beeper or pager. Once you got the beep or page, you had to call back from a payphone, which was 25 cents per call. Man, that was something else back then in the '80s

My Life's Greatest Troubles

and early '90s. We are blessed to have the technology today, so advanced with cell phones, facetime, and other ways to communicate. If I had to stop and use a telephone booth today, I don't think I would because it is more dangerous in today's society. You would probably not stand a chance. Your life is worth too much...please believe it.

While living in Colonial Square Apartments, we got behind on our rent, so we made arrangements with the rental office to get caught up. Rita and I had just started new jobs. I worked in Eastpoint, and Rita worked at the Atlanta Gas Light. Shortly after the rental office agreed to let us pay our rent late, I decided to go check on my mother after dropping Rita off at work. When I got there, my mother told me that my sister Bonita (Neet) was trying to get in touch with me to let me know that Rita and I were being evicted. She said the marshal was sitting our furniture and belongings out on the street. I was, at most, two or three miles away.

When I arrived, they had already gone through our apartment. The movers were putting our belongings out on the street. When I pulled up, people were getting out of their cars and going through and taking our things. My two firearms were stolen, along with the few dollars I had under the rug. I had to stop people from stealing our stuff, so I had to call for help. Thank God the telephone was on. I called Rita at work to let her know what was going on and that I was

My Life's Greatest Troubles

coming to pick her up. I got Charlie, my sister's friend Phil whom we call (Red), to come over and watch my belongings while I got Rita from work.

    Rita had already called her mother and her brother Rod while she was at work, so by the time I picked her up and we got back to our apartment, her mom and brother were pulling up too. My cousin Sharod, brother Andy, Stanley, and Bruce all came to help us put our things back into our apartment. Rod paid the past-due rent for us, so we could get back in our apartment. This was all so crazy because we made a verbal agreement with the landlord to pay the rent the following Friday. However, the Marshall came that Wednesday and evicted us.

CHAPTER 12

*I*t was 1992, and our son was five years old. I was still hustling and still driving my Malibu. Rita and I were about to get married after being together for ten years. We were sweetheart lovers. One Friday in April, when I was selling my cocaine, a quarter ounce for $250.00, one of my friends from school named Pookie came around. Pookie worked at Hubcap Bob.

This Friday, Pookie brought his cousin to buy crack cocaine from me. I tell you, I made a lot of money rolling all day. I knew his cousin Tom for a while, and he bought me out. It had gotten dark by this time, so I decided to shut it down for the night. I wasn't going to sell anything else. It was time to celebrate because Rita and I were getting married that weekend. My brother Andy, Mike, me, and Rita were going to stop by the liquor on the way to my sister Phil's house. We already had some weed, so let the celebration begin.

Pookie's cousin Tom kept paging me back-to-back, wanting to buy more cocaine. I told him I was done for the night and to catch me in the morning, but he insisted that he needed it and would make it worth my while. I trusted him because I went to school with his cousin, so I said OKAY. I agreed to meet him at McDonald's on Cleveland Avenue. I was a little paranoid about meeting him, but I thought I knew him. Tom was not there when I pulled up with Rita, Mike, and Andy. He told me he was going to be in a Camaro.

The Camaro pulled up about three minutes later and parked two cars over from where I was parked. My brother Andy got out to use the pay phone, and Mike went to make the transaction in the Camaro. The next thing I knew, the Tri-City Narcotics undercover agents came from everywhere. They were already in position in the parking lot, and once the deal was done, they surrounded my car with their guns drawn.

Most of them were young white male agents, with two black men and one white female agent. Two white male agents approached the car on the driver's side with a flashlight, and their guns were drawn. One hit me in the mouth with his flashlight and knocked my front tooth out. He told me he didn't mean to hit me in my mouth but not to move. I thank God that it was over thirty years ago when this happened. In this era, the undercover agents would probably have shot and killed Rita and me. They pulled me out of my car, handcuffed me, then put me back in the passenger seat and put Rita in the backseat with another agent. The one who arrested me got in the driver's seat and drove us to College Park Police Department. Tom and Mike rode in the Camaro with another agent, and my brother Andy rode in the truck with another agent.

My Life's Greatest Troubles

The agent driving my car was driving crazy, so I cussed him out, so he increased the speed in the wrong gear. Rita was cussing the agent out too. The agent said the car would be seized, so I would not get it back. I told him hell to the no that they were not getting my car. When we got to the police station, we were booked for possession of a firearm during the commission of a felony, possession of cocaine with intent to distribute, and other felony charges. Tom set me up with the narcotics agents. Once we were booked and in jail, I took the rap for all charges so that Rita and Mike could go home, but they kept Andy and me all weekend. This all happened on Friday, April 3, 1992.

I had to obtain a lawyer. It was someone my auntie Nora knew. His name was Attorney Hartwell, and he came to see me the next day, Saturday. Attorney Hartwell told me that he had to get me out on a bond hearing trial, which may take a while. It was Monday morning, so Andy and I packed up to go to South Fulton County superior court on Stonewall Tell Road in College Park.

We both went before Judge Magistrate to ask to be bound to the superior court of Fulton County, which was a good move. A Magistrate judge cannot give a bond on felony charges. If we were not bound over to the Superior Court, we would stay in jail in College Park until our next court appearance, so we were bound to the Fulton County Jail on Rice Street.

My Life's Greatest Troubles

I had never been locked up, so I was there with my head hung. An inmate asked me what was wrong, and I told him about my charges of possession of cocaine with intent to sell, possession of a weapon during the commission of a felony with no bond, and other charges. He told me to hold my head up. I also told him that my lawyer said it would be a while before he could get the bond. The inmate told me he knew a lawyer who could get us a bond on the charges with no problem. He told us to call Attorney Daniel Kane. I told him thanks and immediately made the collect call to Rita.

I gave her the number to the attorney, and we told each other, "I love you," before hanging up. The next day Rita told me she spoke with the attorney who asked for $500.00, and he would get me a bond by the following Wednesday's bond calendar. That was Monday night, she gave the attorney the money on Tuesday morning, and sure enough, I had a bond on Wednesday. Since I made bond, I got out of jail on Thursday night.

Rita and my sister Zell came and picked me up. God was with me all the way! I really can say that God was on my side. I believe that if it was not for me to get out, it would not have happened even though I know what I was doing was wrong. God will make things happen for you, especially when your life has a purpose. I need to say that I am not perfect in any way, but what I do know is that God is working in my

My Life's Greatest Troubles

favor when I open up to Him in prayer. The evidence shows me that prayer works and that God's protection is real and is displayed even in the midst of disobedience and refusing to obey the close calls on my life. I could have gotten killed by the undercover agents or while in jail, even when the hustle was going down. But God is my refuge and strength and an ever-present help in trouble Psalm 46-1. It is personal to me.

It's Friday, April 10, 1992, and I am out of jail, but my car is in the impound lot in College Park, held by the Tri-City Narcotics. They wanted to seize my 1979 Malibu Classic but no way, Jose. Thank God I had my 1974 Buick Regal, which I just had painted by Leon's Paint shop on Lakewood Avenue. I had it painted royal polo blue from baby blue, a very sharp color. It was the weekend, and Rita and I got married on Sunday evening in Fairburn, Ga. My oldest brother Greg married us. Now I needed to find a job.

The hustle and flow at the time were good, but I loved to work. I got that from my mother because I used to watch her work hard. I needed a job quickly and, in a hurry, so I called my old employer at the Hu-Ray Cleaning Company in Morrow and told him I needed a job. Mr. Ray did not hesitate and told me to come to the shop where he was waiting for me. I got into his red Toyota truck, and he took me to his house, about two to three miles away from the shop. Mr. Ray asked me to clean his swimming pool, pressure wash

My Life's Greatest Troubles

the umbrella and patio furniture, and do some other cleaning in his yard. He even invited me to his house for lunch.

My Life's Greatest Troubles

CHAPTER 13

*I*t was April 13, 1992, and I had my old job back. I went in that Monday evening, and Mr. Ray introduced me to William and said he and I would work together. William and I were cleaning banks and stripping and waxing floors throughout the Atlanta Metropolitan Area. Mr. Ray told William that I was a good worker. William and I were working hard to get it in. I was still hustling, trying to come up with the money to get my 1979 Chevy Malibu out of impound. They were charging me fifteen dollars a day. I needed to retain my lawyer for twenty-five hundred dollars. I tell you, Tri-City did not want me to get my car back. They tried to keep it, but my attorney finally got it back for me, which cost me almost two thousand dollars. They kept my radio system, my speakers, and the whole shebang. It was all good. I was just glad that I was out of jail and working again.

When I got the release of my Malibu classic, I asked one of my mother's neighbors, Mr. Otis Beasley, to take me to get it from the impound lot. I paid him to pull it because the battery was gone, but it was all good. I was just blessed to get it back. I thank God for watching over me through it all. I had just married my girlfriend after ten years of dating. We were living with my mother and had just discovered that my new

My Life's Greatest Troubles

wife was expecting another child.

Rita was still working for the Atlanta Gas Company, and we were about to move to the west side of Atlanta. It is summertime and the first day of July. Time is moving on, and my wife is now six months pregnant with our second son. We moved on July 3, 1992, to Peyton Place in SW Atlanta. I had been working on painting our condominium, pulling up old carpets, and removing window tints before moving in on Independence Day weekend. The next day was the 4th of July, and everyone was celebrating. I got the worst news anyone wants to hear. Mr. Ray called me and told me that William had killed himself. I could not remember if he said last night or this morning because I did not hear it, so Mr. Ray repeated that he shot himself in the head.

Man, I was in shock because I worked with William every day. As a matter of fact, we worked together on Thursday before the holiday. This messed me up because I was in disbelief. I was hurt because I had known William for more than three months. I used to see him around before I worked with him. He loved to wear his hair in a ponytail. Before we started work, he and I would stop and get burgers from Checkers or Rally's. We talked about which burger was the best. I picked Checkers, and he picked Rally's.

William and I had some good times together. Sometimes we would stop by Wendy's and eat for free

My Life's Greatest Troubles

because he had a friend who hooked us up with whatever we wanted to eat. It was said that William killed himself because of his girlfriend whom he lived with. According to rumors, she was going to leave him for someone else. I still don't believe he killed himself. William had other female friends that he talked about. I actually thought some of them were better than the girlfriend he was living with. I do not know what happened in their house, but I don't believe he killed himself. I think someone killed William. I have heard time after time that love will make you do crazy things, and all the trouble and pleasure bring people to do the dumbest things.

I can't imagine shooting myself in the head because of a woman. I was all alone before I met Rita; besides, there are more fish in the sea. Sometimes you have to let go to be able to fish another day. Don't end your life because of a rotten fish. Even if you are a terrible fish, somebody will catch you eventually. You have to live, not die, and pray and trust God that things will get better. These are facts.

Since William was gone, I had to work alone and had a problem with it. Mr. Ray called me and told me to clean the building that William was cleaning until he could get someone to clean them. William had the BFI building in Austell, two exits from where I lived. I was scared to clean the building by myself. I had to go in and figure out how to set the alarm. It always took about an hour to clean that building. I

My Life's Greatest Troubles

kept hearing some weird sounds. The BFI driver would come in while I was cleaning the building, and it would scare the crap out of me. Sometimes I could hear William talking and laughing. It was very spooky, so I started taking Mike Mike with me.

Mike Mike was Mr. Otis's nephew from back in my mother's neighborhood. William cleaned the Kroger Warehouse on Oakleigh Dr. in East Point. I had to start going to work at 4 o'clock to get the company van to drive because I had to pick up another co-worker named Larry. He lived in Morrow but did not have a driver's license. We worked together, stripping, waxing, and buffing floors. Every day before we started, we would stop and eat at Morrison's Cafeteria at the State Farmers Market in Forest Park. We also did the floors at Chapman Drug Pharmacy on Central, Cole Concrete Products on Moreland in Conley, and Bishop Brothers Auto Auction on Metropolitan Parkway, once known as "Stewart Avenue." Stewart Avenue was named after Andrew P. Stewart. It was changed in 1997 because the area was a red-light district and had a reputation for prostitution activities.

One night while Larry and I were out working, we saw some prostitutes walking up the hill to the motel across the street from Bishop Brothers Auto Auction. I drove over to check it out, but I tell you without a doubt that some of them were undercover cops dressed up like prostitutes. We decided that

My Life's Greatest Troubles

there was nothing wrong with looking, so as I went up the hill to the back of the motel, oh s$%%, I said (wow), APD was all posted up in there (man). I thought I was in some more trouble just because I knew I had some weed on me, Larry had beer, and I was the driver. If you are wondering what APD means: Atlanta Police Department. They asked us what we were doing there, and I had to think fast. I told them I was trying to find a building called Bishop Brother because we were supposed to strip and wax the floor. The officer shined the flashlight in the back of the company van and noticed the equipment. They told me to get out of there and told us the building was across the street and don't come back up there. I said okay and thanked the officer(wow). I was sweating because I thought they smelled marijuana in the company van. Talk about being paranoid! I thought I was about to catch another court case, and I had not yet gone to court with Tri-City Narcotics. Again, God was looking out for me!

Question? Do you think we were lucky? Some may say yes, but I say no. Back in 1992, I would have said I got lucky or caught a break. As I think about all the close calls in my life and reminisce about writing this novel about "My Life's Greatest Troubles," it made me realize that God has always been right there, even when I was not thinking about Him or serving Him. It wasn't luck; it was God's grace and His unmerited favor because I got something I did not deserve. God's grace is the unmerited favor. God's grace and mercy follow me all day, even in the midst of disobedience and my mess and troubles. I thank God. Mr. Ray kept adding more jobs to the list of what he wanted me to clean. Five nights a week, we cleaned and buffed the Family and Children Dentistry on Fairburn Rd, and First Baptist Church of Conley, which is now Wings of Faith Worldwide Ministries.

A lot had already happened that year. We moved to Peyton Place, got married, caught a drug charge, and were expecting our second child. I received a summons to appear in the Fulton County Superior Court on July 30. I was being charged with purchase/possession of a controlled substance/first offender act, possession of a firearm or knife during commission/attempt/ first offenders act dangerous drugs. I ended up being sentenced under the First Offenders Act and got 10 years' probation along with the $750 fine.

I had to report to my probation officer Mrs. Floyd in person until my fine was paid off in full. I reported to Mrs. Floyd three times. She told me that I could pay the fine in full at any time because I would not have to report to her if I did that. However, Mrs. Floyd told me that my probation still stands for the number of years that I was sentenced. I could not have any weapon or drugs on me or around me, and there were other things she said I could not do while on probation.

My Life's Greatest Troubles

I had to report once a month, and she gave me a drug test when I reported on the second month (wow). I failed the drug test because I knew I had been smoking marijuana like a 55 Chevy with a blown head gasket. Mrs. Floyd said to me that my pee was dirty. That is how she said it because my pee was contaminated with drugs. Mrs. Floyd asked if I wanted to talk about it, and I said no, there was nothing to talk about because I did smoke. She told me thank you for being honest. She then said she would see me next month, so I said thank you and left. Here it is again, with God's favor on my life as He looked beyond my fault. Mrs. Floyd could have put me in a motion to revoke my probation, but God was on my side. It had nothing to do with Mrs. Floyd because everything that happened to me was because of God's favor. I paid my fine in full and didn't have to report every month anymore. Life goes on! I was still making money working hard for Hu-Ray Cleaning Company, and we were still living at Peyton Village Condominiums. I loved the peace and quiet.

It was early fall in October 1992, around the 8th. I was at home chilling with my wife and son Vernon Jr. (Torrence), and Mike Mike was visiting with us. Rita was due to deliver our baby any day. On this particular day, my wife Rita was in the kitchen frying some chicken after she gave Vernon Jr. his bath and put him to bed. Rita was starting to hurt, so we called the doctor's office. He advised that I take her to Crawford Long Hospital in Midtown. We got Vernon

My Life's Greatest Troubles

Jr. up, dressed him, and took him to my mother, and Mike Mike and I took Rita to the hospital. We called my mother-in-law and her friend Mr. Henry to meet us at the hospital. We were all there. The staff wanted Rita to walk up and down the hallway after they admitted her overnight. Around 2pm on October 9, 1992, Rita was about to give birth, and Dr. Lightfoot was running late, but he showed up in the nick of time, and our son was born at 2:30pm on Friday, October 9, 1992. He weighed 6 lbs. 10 oz., and we named him Verderius Marquae Jackson Smith. I was happy everything went well with my wife Rita and our newborn son Verderius. At the end of the month, my father and stepmother came over to visit and see their new grandson Verderius.

I was still working hard for the Hu-Ray company, and the Thanksgiving and Christmas holidays are here. It was our first holiday in our place at the Peyton Village Condominium. It was time to take Christmas pictures of the boys, so we took them to Kmart on Cleveland Ave. Vernon Jr. is six now, and Verderius is 2 1/2 months old.

My Life's Greatest Troubles

What a year it had been. A lot of things happened in 1992. I thank God for everything that happened. It started in April when I caught a drug case and married my girlfriend of ten years. I got my job back with Hu-Ray Cleaning Company, and my co-worker William killed himself. I almost caught another case by being in the wrong place at the wrong time when I should have been at work. The biggest blessing was when we welcomed our second son into the world in October. What an amazing journey.

As I conclude "My life's Greatest Troubles," part one, everything in this novel is valid in

My Life's Greatest Troubles

accordance with the facts and reality of my true story. I thank God for allowing me all the experiences, encounters, and contact with facts because of the painful experiences which gave me the knowledge of doing, seeing, and feeling. Though painful at times, don't get it twisted; I am proud of the deep pleasure and satisfaction resulting from my achievements. Am I glad, mad, or sad? No way is there anyone to blame. Do I want sympathy? No, I do not. It is what it is, "My life's Greatest Troubles." Part 2 will take twists and turns in 1993, and it will pick up there, so stay tuned by yours truly, Vernon Smith, Sr.

My Life's Greatest Troubles

My mother and father

My Life's Greatest Troubles

My Life's Greatest Troubles

EPILOGUE
My Life's Greatest Troubles Part 2
The Story Continues
2023

I asked her what her name was, and she said her name was Ciara. I said, " Okay, Ciara, I'm V she said okay, V, what's your real name, I said Vernon, but call me V, and your friend's name? Ciara says my friend's name is Lexus. Ciara was cool. Her friend Lexus was at the Krystal's waiting on us to pull up. I gave Ciara my pager number, and we became friends.

After we talked and started hanging out, I found out later that Ciara and Lexus had a bet with each other that Ciara was going to ride in Dookie; Dookie was the name I called my truck. Well, Ciara won the bet she rode in Dookie. Ciara lived in Decatur on the east of Atlanta, where it's "greater," the girl was "badddd," and her friend Lexus was no joke.

I'm all in the hotels... at the Holiday Inn on Old Dixie Highway (one of my main spots) or the Ramada Inn on Fulton Industrial Boulevard. Man, I had a blast in the past. I would meet other friends at the skating rink, Deja, Angel, Kiki, Shamika, and Ramonda from the south side of Atlanta. Ramonda lived in Crosby Hill and worked for McDonald's in Forest Park. I got free meals every day, lol. Man, I had even met this pretty fine chick in DeKalb County. She lived in the

My Life's Greatest Troubles

East Hampton Apartments, and her name was Mika.

We met at the shopping mall. Yes, SIR...she had her own apartment! I'm all in the Hamptons, man I definitely had no business out there. One night I went to hang out with Mika to smoke and chill before I had to head back to the Southside. I had a few extra bags of weed on me but not much, maybe five or six extra bags because I don't trap out of my truck. I was parked in the apartments in Dookie as Mika and I were smoking. I told Mika I was going out to sell the few sacks of weed I had on me.

I didn't have my road dog with me because he was waiting for me to pick him up on the south side of Atlanta. Next thing I know, DeKalb County Blackjacks is pulling up in the complex. They jumped out of their cars, laying everybody down with their guns drawn. Some took off running, including me. I was in the midst of all this, I thought. The Blackjacks were the narcotics police for DeKalb County, just like the Atlanta Red Dogs are the narcotic cops for Atlanta. I said oh s*** I ran into the stairwell of a unit.

The Blackjack cops were busting the complex, and I was all out there! I didn't know anybody that lived out here other than Mika, and I was away from her unit. I had some sacks of weed on me, so I threw them down somewhere. I was lying down in the stairway, and all I could hear was the Blackjacks running and talking on their walkie-talkie radios. This

My Life's Greatest Troubles

female opened her door and saw me lying in the stairway. I did not know her, and she did not know me, but she told me to come in. She was my angel! I was scared. The weed I had on me, I had thrown down. Still, I could have gotten caught, had my truck impounded, and gone to jail in Dekalb County while I was already on probation in Fulton County. How was I going to explain this to my wife?

God was with me for sure! I know it because when this female heard the commotion outside and opened her door, she could have closed it and left me there. She was nice enough to invite me into her apartment, so I had to break her off a little "something, you know...break bread." I waited until everything had cooled down. Boy, I tell you, V, you hell, man. They had the drug dogs and the helicopter. Dekalb ain't nothing to play around with. After thanking the female for rescuing me, I returned to Mika's unit to tell her what had happened. She already knew they were busting the apartment unit. Mika said, V, they do this on a regular. I said, hell no, it's time for me to get back to the south side of Atlanta. That was enough for me...

My Life's Greatest Troubles

ABOUT THE AUTHOR

Vernon T. Smith Sr. is an Anointed Author and a family man who has experienced a personal walk with GOD through his journey of life. He was born and raised in the red hills of Atlanta Georgia. A man of faith and strong conviction. His driven passion demonstrates unconditional love to his family, friends, and the community. GOD'S love is forever and will remain deep in my heart.

My Life's Greatest Troubles

I pray that this book, My Life's Greatest Troubles, will help to heal, empower, and encourage.

Nothing can be compared to Vernon's great, spiritual awakening. Vernon discovered his life's purpose and joy to share his story to the world because in his heart, he knows you must put GOD in everything. Vernon is continually amazed how "his life's greatest troubles" has changed, strengthened and given him hope when all seemed lost. Vernon prays that his books reaches and touches the HEART of men all over the world.

Feel free to contact Vernon at vernonsmitht.vs@gmail.com or follow him on Facebook https://www.facebook.com/vernon.smith.7146557

My Life's Greatest Troubles

www.ingramcontent.com/pod-product-compliance
Lightning Source LLC
Chambersburg PA
CBHW072126160426
43198CB00030B/2316